National Legal Kit

Simplified Family Legal Forms

by Daniel Sitarz
Attorney-at-Law

Nova Publishing Company
Small Business and Consumer Legal Books and Software
Carbondale, Illinois

Comsewogue Public Library
170 Terryville Road
Port Jefferson Station, NY 11776

© 2012 Daniel Sitarz

All rights reserved. This publication may not be reproduced in whole or in part by any means without prior written consent. Editorial assistance by Janet Harris Sitarz and Melanie Bray. Manufactured in the United States.

ISBN 978-1-892949-57-8   Book ($19.95)

Cataloging-in-Publication Data
   Sitarz, Dan, 1948-
      Simplified Family Legal Forms Kit / by Daniel Sitarz. -- 3rd ed.--Carbondale, ILL.:
         Nova Publishing Company, 2012
      160 p. cm. -- (National Legal Kit series).
      1. Forms (Law)—United States—Popular Works. 2. Civil Law—United States—Forms.
      I. Sitarz, Daniel. II. Title. III. Series.
      ISBN 978-1-892949-57-8   Book ($19.95).

Nova Publishing Company is dedicated to providing up-to-date and accurate legal information to the public. All Nova publications are periodically revised to contain the latest available legal information.

3rd Edition; 1st Printing	February, 2012
2nd Edition; 1st Printing	February, 2008
1st Edition; 2nd Printing	October, 2006
1st Edition; 1st Printing	September, 2005

This publication is designed to provide accurate and authoritative information in regard to the subject matter covered. It is sold with the understanding that the publisher and author are not engaged in rendering legal, accounting, or other professional services. If legal advice or other expert assistance is required, the services of a competent professional person should be sought.

—From a Declaration of Principles jointly adopted by a Committee of the American Bar Association and a Committee of Publishers

DISCLAIMER AND WARNING: Any Nova legal product, whether book, CD, kit, or individual legal form should only be a starting point for you and should not be used nor relied upon without consulting with an attorney first. Nova legal products are not intended as a substitute for legal advice. Nova legal products contains the basic terms and language that should be included in similar legal documents. However, laws vary from time to time and from state to state. State law should be reviewed to determine which current law is applicable and to determine the existence of any state-specific requirements. Purchasers and persons intending to use this any Nova legal product for the preparation of any legal document are advised to check specifically on the current applicable laws in any jurisdiction in which they intend the documents to be effective. Although Nova Publishing Company and its authors try to keep Nova legal products accurate and up-to-date, the accuracy of any of these products can not be guaranteed. Because of differing interpretations of law in different jurisdictions and possible unanticipated changes in governing statutes and case law relating to the application of any information contained in any Nova legal product, the author, publisher, and any and all persons or entities involved in any way in the preparation, publication, sale, or distribution of this book disclaim all responsibility for the legal effects or consequences of any document prepared or action taken in reliance upon information contained in any Nova product. These legal products are provided 'as-is'. No representations or warranties either express or implied, are made or given regarding suitability, merchantability, fitness for a particular purpose, or completeness for your particular purpose, nor regarding the legal consequences of a particular use of any information contained in any Nova legal product. The materials are used at your own risk. Neither Nova Publishing Company, nor its authors, shall be responsible or liable for any direct or indirect, incidental, special, exemplary, or consequential damages (including, but not limited to, procurement of substitute goods or services; loss of use, data, or profits; or business interruption) however used, and on any theory of liability whatsoever, whether in contract, strict liability or tort (including negligence or otherwise) arising in any way out of the use of any Nova legal product or materials. Nova legal products are not printed, published, sold, circulated, or distributed with the intention that it be used to procure or aid in the procurement of any legal effect or ruling in any jurisdiction in which such procurement or aid may be restricted by statute.

Nova Publishing Green Business Policies

Nova Publishing Company takes seriously the impact of book publishing on the Earth and its resources. Nova Publishing Company is committed to protecting the environment and to the responsible use of natural resources. As a book publisher, with paper as a core part of our business, we are very concerned about the future of the world's remaining endangered forests and the environmental impacts of paper production. We are committed to implementing policies that will support the preservation of endangered and ancient forests globally and to advancing 'best practices' within the book and paper industries. Our company's policy is to print all of our books on 100% recycled paper, with 100% post-consumer waste content, de-inked in a chlorine-free process. In addition, all Nova Publishing Company books are printed using soy-based inks. As a result of these environmental policies, Nova Publishing Company has saved hundreds of thousands of gallons of water, hundreds of thousands of kilowatts of electricity, thousand of pounds of pollution and carbon dioxide, and thousands of trees that would otherwise have been used in the traditional manner of publishing its books. Nova Publishing Company is very proud to be one of the first members of the Green Press Initiative, a nonprofit program dedicated to supporting publishers in their efforts to reduce their use of fiber obtained from endangered forests. (see www.greenpressinitiative.org). Nova Publishing Company is also proud to be an initial signatory on the Book Industry Treatise on Responsible Paper Use. In addition, Nova Publishing Company uses all compact fluorescent lighting; recycles all office paper products, aluminum and plastic beverage containers, and printer cartridges; uses 100% post-consumer fiber, process-chlorine-free, acid-free paper for 95% of in-house paper use; and, when possible, uses electronic equipment that is EPA Energy Star-certified. Nova's freight shipments are coordinated to minimize energy use whenever possible. Finally, all carbon emissions from Nova Publishing Company office energy use are offset by the purchase of wind-energy credits that are used to subsidize the building of wind turbines (see www.nativeenergy.com). We strongly encourage other publishers and all partners in publishing supply chains to adopt similar policies.

Nova Publishing Company
Small Business and Consumer Legal Books and Software
1103 West College St.
Carbondale, IL 62901
Editorial: (800) 748-1175
www.novapublishing.com

Distributed by:
National Book Network
4501 Forbes Blvd., Suite 200
Lanham, MD 20706
Orders: (800) 462-6420

Table of Contents

Using Legal Forms 4
   How to Use This Book 5
   Installation Instructions for the Forms-on-CD ... 5
   Additional Material Included on Forms-on-CD . 5

Contracts 6
   Contract 6
   Extension of Contract 6
   Modification of Contract 7
   Termination of Contract 7
   Contract Exhibit 7

Powers of Attorney 7
   Unlimited Power of Attorney 8
   Limited Power of Attorney 8
   Durable Unlimited Power of Attorney for Financial Affairs (Effective Immediately) 8
   Durable Unlimited Power of Attorney for Financial Affairs (Effective on Disability)............. 8
   Durable Health Care Power of Attorney 9
   Revocation of Power of Attorney 9

Last Will and Testament 9
   Property Instructions 10
   Beneficiary Instructions 11
   Preparing Your Will 12
   Will for Person with Children........................ 16
   Will with No Children................................... 16
   Completing and Signing Your Will 17

Living Wills 18
   Preparing and Signing a Living Will 18
   Revocation of Living Will 19

Advance Health Care Directives (CD only) .. 20
   Preparing and Signing an Advance Health
      Care Directive 21

Living Trusts 22
   Living Trust 23
   Schedule of Assets of Living Trust 23
   Schedule of Beneficiaries of Living Trust 23
   Assignment to Living Trust 23
   Amendment of Living Trust 23
   Revocation of Living Trust 23

Releases 23
   General Release 24
   Mutual Release 24
   Specific Release 24

Receipts 24
   Receipt in Full 24
   Receipt on Account 24
   Receipt for Goods 25

Leases of Real Estate 25
   Residential Lease 25
   Month-to-Month Rental Agreement 26
   Amendment of Lease 26
   Extension of Lease 27
   Sublease 27
   Consent to Sublease of Lease 27
   Notice of Breach of Lease 27
   Notice of Rent Default 27
   Notice to Vacate Property 27
   Notice to Terminate Lease 27
   Receipt for Lease Security Deposit 28
   Rent Receipt 28

Rental of Personal Property 28
   Personal Property Rental Agreement 28

Sale of Personal Property 28
   Contract for Sale of Personal Property 28
   Bill of Sale, with Warranties 28
   Bill of Sale, without Warranties 29
   Bill of Sale, Subject to Debt 29

Sale of Real Estate 29
   Agreement to Sell Real Estate 29
   Option to Buy Real Estate Agreement 30
   Quitclaim Deed 30
   Warranty Deed 31

Promissory Notes 31
   Promissory Note (Installment Repayment) 31
   Promissory Note (Lump Sum Repayment) 32
   Promissory Note (On Demand) 32
   Release of Promissory Note 32

Using Legal Forms

This book provides individuals with a set of legal forms that have been prepared with the problems and normal transactions of everyday life in mind. The contracts and other various legal documents that are used in this book are written in plain English. These forms are intended to be used in those situations that are clearly described by the specific terms of the particular form. Of course, while most transactions will fall within the bounds of these normal situations, some legal circumstances will present non-standard situations. The forms in this book are designed to be readily adaptable to most usual situations. They may be carefully altered to conform to the particular transaction that you may be confronted with. However, if you are faced with a complex or tangled legal situation, the advice of a competent lawyer is highly recommended. It may also be advisable to create your legal document for a certain legal situation and have a lawyer check it for any local legal circumstances. The proper and cautious use of the forms provided in this book will allow the typical person to save considerable money on legal costs. Perhaps more importantly, these forms will provide a method for the person to avoid costly misunderstandings about what exactly was intended in a particular situation or transaction.

How to Use This Book

In each section of this book, you will find an introductory section that will give you an overview of the types of situations in which the forms in that section will generally be used. Following that overview, there will be a brief explanation of the specific uses for each form. Included in the information provided for each form will be a discussion of the legal terms and conditions provided in the form. Finally, for each form, there is a listing of the information that must be compiled to complete the form. You may then turn to the back section of the book. In this section, the forms are all provided in the same order as they are presented in the table of contents. All of the forms in the back section of this book are perforated for easy tear-out use. All of the forms are also provided on the enclosed CD in both customizable text and fillable PDF formats. Most of the forms in this book will be valid if you simply 'fill in the blanks' on the tear-out forms in the back of the book. There are a few exceptions: You are strongly advised to retype the will forms and the living will forms following the instructions that are contained in those sections (or use the forms that are provided on the CD). For these extremely important documents, it is important that you have a clean, clear original document that will be accepted by judges, courts, family members, and others who may need to feel assured that the document has been prepared with careful thought and attention to detail.

IMPORTANT NOTE: Also provided only on the CD are several appendices of state-specific laws relating to powers of attorney, estate planning, and real esate laws. Before using any of the forms in this kit, you are strongly advised to carefully check the appropriate appendix listing for your state, for the particular topic, to see if there are any specific state requirements that must be met regarding the use of a specific form.

In addition to the tear-out forms that are shown in this instruction book and their corresponding text and PDF forms on the CD, a number of state-specific legal forms for certain situations are provided only on the CD. The topics for these state-specific forms are: powers of attorney, advance health care directives, and real estate disclosures. In most cases, you may choose to use the standard generic form that is provided in the book and on the CD or choose to use the state-specific form for your state. In a few situations, you must use the state-specific form that is provided. Please check the appendix listing for your particular state for the specific topic for more detailed information and instructions. It is recommended that you review the table of contents of this book in order to gain a broad overview of the range and type of legal documents that are available. Then, before you prepare any of the forms for use, you should carefully read the introductory information and instructions in the section containing the particular form that you wish to use. Try to be as detailed and specific as possible as you fill in these forms. The more precise the description, the less likelihood that later disputes may develop over what was actually intended by the language chosen.If in doubt as to whether a particular form will work in a specific application or if you are at all unsure of the use or consequences of a particular form, please consult a competent lawyer.

Installation Instructions for the Forms-on-CD

Quick-Start Installation for PCs
① Insert the enclosed CD in your computer.
② The installation program will start automatically. Follow the onscreen prompts and make your choices.
③ If the CD installation does not start automatically, click on START, then RUN, then BROWSE, and select your CD drive, and then select the file "Install.exe." Finally, click OK to run the installation program.
④ During the installation program, you will be prompted as to whether or not you wish to install the Adobe Acrobat Reader® program. If you do not already have the Adobe Acrobat Reader® program installed on your hard drive, you will need to select the full installation that will install this program to your computer.
⑤ There is a 'read-me' PDF document on the CD. It contains instructions for preparing the text and PDF forms.

Installation Instructions for MACs®
① Insert the enclosed CD in your computer.
② Copy the folder "Forms for Macs" to your hard drive. All of the PDF and text-only forms are included in this folder.
③ If you do not already have the Adobe Acrobat Reader® program installed on your hard drive, you will need to download the version of this software that is appropriate for you particular MAC operating system from www.adobe.com. Note: The latest versions of the MAC operating system (OS-X) has PDF capabilities built into it.
④ There is a 'read-me' PDF document on the CD. It contains instructions for preparing the text and PDF forms.

Additional Material Included on Forms-on-CD-(Refer to and use if necessary)

Read-Me.pdf (This document contains instructions for using the forms on the CD)
Appendix: State Estate Planning Laws
Appendix: State Real Esate Laws
Appendix: State Power of Attorney Laws
Property Questionnaire (Found under Last Will and Testament; may also be used for Living Trusts)
Beneficiary Questionaiare (Found under Last Will and Testament; may also be used for Living Trusts)
California Notary Acknowledgement (Residents of California must use this Notary Acknowledgement on all
    forms that require notarization if the form is intended to be legal in the State of California)
State-specific Advance Health Care Directives (for all states)
State-specific Durable Powers of Attorney (Only 18 states provide state-specific forms-See Power of Attorney appendix)
Pennsylvania Power of Attorney Addendum
State-specific Real Estate Disclosures (Only 32 states requre such a form)
Addendum to Lease (California)
Addendum to Lease (Chicago)
Chicago Heating Disclosure Form
Chicago Residential Landlord and Tenant Ordinance Summary
New York Notice of Assignment (to Living Trust)
Registration of Living Trust (See Estate Planning Appendix)
California Addendum to Real Estate Contract

Contracts

The foundation of most agreements is a contract. A *contract* is merely an agreement by which two or more parties each promise to do something. This simple definition of a contract can encompass incredibly complex agreements. The objective of a good contract is to clearly set out the terms of the agreement. Once the parties have reached an oral understanding of what their agreement should be, the terms of the deal should be put in writing. Contrary to what many attorneys may tell you, the written contract should be clearly written and easily understood by both parties to the agreement. It should be written in precise and unambiguous terms. The most common causes for litigation over contracts are arguments over the meaning of the language used. Remember that both sides of the agreement should be able to understand and agree to the language being used.

A contract has to have certain prerequisites to be enforceable in court. These requirements are relatively simple and most will be present in any standard agreement. However, you should understand what the various legal requirements are before you prepare your own contracts. To be enforceable, a contract must have *consideration*. In the context of contract law, this simply means that both parties to the contract must have promised to do something or forego taking some type of action. If one of the parties has not promised to do anything or forego any action, he or she will not be able to legally force the other party to comply with the terms of the contract. There has to be some form of mutual promise for a contract to be valid. For example: Andy agrees to pay Bill if Bill paints a car. Andy's promise is to pay Bill if the job is completed. Bill's promise is to paint the car. If Bill paints the car and is not paid, Andy's promise to pay Bill can be enforced in court. Similarly, if Bill fails to paint the car, Andy can have the contract enforced in court. Andy and Bill's mutual promises are the consideration necessary to have a valid and enforceable contract.

Another requirement is that the parties to the contract be clearly identified and the terms of the contract also be clearly spelled out. The terms and description need not be complicated, but they must be spelled out in enough detail to enable the parties to the contract (and any subsequent court) to clearly determine what exactly the parties were referring to when they made the contract. In the prior example, the names and addresses of the parties must be included for the contract to be enforceable. In addition, a description of the car must be incorporated in the contract. Finally, a description of the type of paint job and the amount of money to be paid should also be contained in the contract.

The following documents are included for use in situations requiring a basic contract. There are documents for modifying, extending, and terminating a basic contract. A form for adding exhibits to a contract is also included. *Note*: If you are at all unsure of the correct use of any forms in this section, please consult a competent attorney.

Contract: This basic document can be adapted for use in many situations. The terms of the contract that the parties agree to should be carefully spelled out and inserted where indicated. The other information that is required are the names and addresses of the parties to the contract and the date the contract is to take effect. This basic contract form is set up to accommodate an agreement between two individuals. If a business is party to the contract, please identify the name and type of business entity (for example: Jackson Car Stereo, a New York sole proprietorship, etc.) in the first section of the contract.

Extension of Contract: This document should be used to extend the effective time period during which a contract is in force. The use of this form allows the time limit to be extended without having to entirely redraft the contract. Under this document, all of the other terms of the contract will remain the same, with only the expiration date changing. You will need to fill in both the original expiration date and the new expiration date. Other information necessary will be the names and addresses of the parties to the contract and a description of the contract. A copy of the original contract should be attached to this form.

Modification of Contract: Use this form to modify any other terms of a contract (other than the expiration date). The modification can be used to change any portion of the contract. Simply note what changes are being made in the appropriate place on this form. If a portion of the contract is being deleted, make note of the deletion. If certain language is being substituted, state the substitution clearly. If additional language is being added, make this clear. For example, you may wish to use language as follows:

- "Paragraph _____ is deleted from this contract."
- "The following new paragraph is added to this contract:"

A copy of the original contract should be attached to this form.

Termination of Contract: This document is intended to be used when both parties to a contract mutually desire to end the contract prior to its original expiration date. Under this form, both parties agree to release each other from any claims against each other based on anything in the contract. This document effectively ends any contractual arrangement between two parties. Information necessary to complete this form are the names and addresses of the parties to the contract, a description of the contract, and the effective date of the termination of the contract.

Contract Exhibit: This form may be used with any contract. It provides a simple method for attaching other documents to the contract and having them considered as a legal part of the contract. If you have documents, letters, forms, etc. that you feel are necessary to have as a part of a contract, use this simple form. The space after "Exhibit" in the title of this document is for placing a letter to describe this exhibit (for example: Exhibit A). In the space provided, describe clearly which particular contract the exhibit is to be attached to (for example: The Contract dated June 1, 2004, between John Smith of 111 Main St., Uptown, NY and Mary Johnson of 222 Broadway Ave., Downtown, CA).

Powers of Attorney

A *power of attorney* form is a document that is used to allow one person to give the authority to act on his or her behalf to another person. The person signing the power of attorney grants legal authority to another person to "stand in his or her shoes" and act legally for him or her. The person who receives the power of attorney is called an *attorney-in-fact*. However, this title and the power of attorney form does *not* mean that the person receiving the power has to be a lawyer. Power of attorney forms are useful documents for many occasions. They can be used to authorize someone else to sign certain documents if you cannot be present when the signatures are necessary. For example, a real estate closing in another state can be completed without your presence by providing a power of attorney to a real estate agent (or even a friend) that authorizes him or her to sign the documents on your behalf. Similarly, if you must be away from your home on a trip, and certain actions must be made in your absence, a power of attorney may be granted to enable another person to legally perform on your behalf. The form can also be used to allow your accountant to negotiate with the IRS, allow your secretary to sign checks and temporarily operate your business, or for many other purposes.

Traditionally, property matters were the type of actions handled with powers of attorney. Increasingly, however, people are using a specific type of power of attorney to authorize other persons to act on their behalf in the event of disability. This broad type of power of attorney is called a *durable power of attorney*. A durable power of attorney is intended to remain in effect even if a person becomes disabled or incompetent. All states have passed legislation that specifically authorizes this type of power of attorney. Two of the durable power of attorney forms that are included in this book are intended to be used to allow another person to handle financial matters for an incapacitated person. A durable power of attorney designed to handle financial affairs can be prepared to operate in two separate situations: first, to be effective immediately and remain in effect if you become disabled, or second, to only go into effect *if* you become disabled. Both durable power of attorney for financial affairs forms require notarization of the forms and the use of two witnesses to the signature, even though this in not a technical requirement in all states. The use of a notary public and witnesses will generally prevent delays or challenges to the powers that are granted in the durable power of attorney. Please note that the two durable power of attorney for financial affairs forms that are included in this kit can not be used to make healthcare decisions on behalf of another person. The legal form that allows another person to make various healthcare decisions on behalf of an incapacitated person is referred to as a *durable healthcare power of attorney*. This type of form only goes into effect if you are unable to communicate your wishes and that incapacity is certified by an attending physician. It is also included in this kit and discussed below. *Note*: Powers of attorney are very powerful legal documents. They can be used to grant virtually unlimited legal power to another person. You are advised to proceed with caution when using any of these forms. If you have any questions regarding their use, please consult a competent attorney. Note also that some financial institutions may require that you complete their own particular power of attorney form for transaction with their institution. Note also that the CD contains many state-specific Durable Powers of Attorney. Before using any of these forms, please check the Appendix of State Power of Attorney Laws under the listing for your state (also on the CD).

Unlimited Power of Attorney: This form should be used only in situations where you desire to authorize another person to act for you in *all* transactions. The grant of power under this document is unlimited. All that is necessary are the names and addresses of both the person granting the power and the person receiving the power. Both persons should sign the document. The signature of the person granting the power should be notarized and witnessed by two people. The attorney-in-fact should also sign the Acknowledgement and Acceptance section of this form. NOTE: Because of the length of this form, it is only inluded on the CD (as both text and PDF files).

Limited Power of Attorney: This document provides for a *limited* grant of authority to another person. It should be used in those situations when you need to authorize another person to act for you in a specific manner or to perform a specific action. The type of acts that you authorize the other person to perform should be spelled out in detail to avoid confusion (for example, to sign any necessary forms to complete the closing of the sale of real estate). What is needed to complete this form are the names and addresses of the person granting the power and the person receiving the power, and a full and detailed description of the powers granted. Both persons should sign the document. The signature of the person granting the power should be notarized and witnessed by two people.

Durable Unlimited Power of Attorney for Financial Affairs (Effective Immediately): Like the Unlimited Power of Attorney described above, this form should be used only in a situation in which you desire to authorize another person to act for you in *all* transactions. The grant of power under this document is unlimited. However, unlike the general Unlimited Power of Attorney, this form becomes effective immediately, *and* remains fully in effect even if you later become incapacitated or disabled. This broad grant of power will be effective to allow your attorney-in-fact to perform on your behalf both now and in the event of your disability. To complete this form, the name and address of the person granting the power and also of the person receiving the power should be filled in. Both persons should sign the document. The signature of the person granting the power should be notarized and witnessed by two other persons at the same time. The person receiving the power of attorney cannot be one of the witnesses.

Durable Unlimited Power of Attorney for Financial Affairs (Effective on Disability): Like the Unlimited Power of Attorney described above, this form should be used only in a situation in which you desire to authorize another person to act for you in *all* transactions. The grant of power under this document is unlimited. However, unlike the general Unlimited Power of Attorney, this form *only* becomes effective if you are incapacitated or disabled, and such incapacitation is certified by an attending physician. This broad grant of power will be effective to allow your attorney-in-fact to perform on your behalf *only* in the event of your disability. To complete this form, the name and address of the person granting the power and also of the person receiving the power should be filled in. Both persons should sign the document. The signature of the person granting the power should be notarized and witnessed by two other persons at the same time. The person receiving the power of attorney cannot be one of the witnesses.

Durable Health Care Power of Attorney: This document is not effective for use in any financial situations. Rather, it is designed to authorize another to make decisions on your behalf in the event that you are unable to make such decisions yourself, such as if you are unconscious. This document will only take effect upon a person becoming unable to manage his or her own affairs, and only after this incapacitation has been certified by an attending physician. The person appointed will then have the authority to view your medical records, consult with your doctors and make any required decisions regarding your health care. This document may be carefully tailored to fit your needs and concerns and can be used in conjunction with a living will. It is already part of an Advance Health Care Directive (discussed later), so if you complete that document you need not additionally complete this form. To complete this form, the name and address of the person granting the power and also of the person receiving the power should be filled in. You may also add additional instructions or conditions if you wish. Both persons should sign the document. The signature of the person granting the power should be notarized and witnessed by two other persons at the same time. The person receiving the power of attorney cannot be one of the witnesses. There are also other restrictions on who may be a witness and these are clearly noted in the form in the Witness Attestation section.

Revocation of Power of Attorney: This document may be used with any of the above five power of attorney forms. The revocation is used to terminate the original authority that was granted to the other person in the first place. If the grant of power was for a limited purpose and that purpose is complete, this revocation should be used as soon after the transaction as possible. In any event, if you choose to revoke a power of attorney, a copy of this revocation should be provided to the person to whom the power was given. Copies should also be given to any party that may have had dealings with the attorney-in-fact before the revocation and to any party with whom the attorney-in-fact may be expected to attempt to deal with after the revocation. If used to revoke a durable health care power of attorney, make sure you provide a copy of the revocation to your primary physician and a health care facility if you are a resident.

Last Will and Testament

A *will* (or *Last Will and Testament*) is a legal document that, when accepted by a probate court, is proof of an intent to transfer property to the persons or organizations named in the will upon the death of the maker of the will. The maker of the will is known as the *testator*. A will is effective for the transfer of property that is owned by the testator upon his or her death. A will can be changed, modified, or revoked at any time by the testator prior to his or her death. It is equally important to understand that in order for a will to be valid, it must generally be prepared, witnessed, and signed according to certain technical legal procedures. Although a will is perfectly valid if it is written in plain English and does not use technical legal language, it *must* be prepared, witnessed, and signed in the manner outlined in this book. This cannot be overemphasized. You cannot take any shortcuts when following the instructions as they relate to the procedures necessary for completing and signing your will. These procedures are not at all difficult and consist generally of carefully preparing your will in the manner outlined later in this section, signing it in the manner specified, and having three witnesses and a notary public also sign the document. (Although not a legal requirement, the notarization of your will can aid in its proof of existence in court later, if necessary). Before you begin to actually prepare your own will, you must understand what your assets are, who your beneficiaries are to be, and what your personal desires are as to how those assets should be distributed among your beneficiaries. The following discussions on property and beneficiaries will assist you in this task.

Note: In some cases (for example, those involving extremely complicated business or personal financial holdings, those that involve the desire to create a complex trust arrangement, or if you are unsure of the correct use of any of the will forms in this book), it is clearly advisable to consult an attorney for the preparation of your will. However, in most circumstances and for most people, the terms of a will that will provide for the necessary protection are relatively routine and may be safely prepared without the added expense of consulting a lawyer.

Property Instructions

In general, by using a will, you can bequeath any property that you own at the time of your death. However, there are forms of property that you may "own," but which may not be transferred by way of a will. In addition, you may own only a percentage or share of certain other property. In such situations, only that percentage or share that you actually own may be left by your will. Finally, there are types of property ownership that are automatically transferred to another party at your death, regardless of the presence of a will.

In the first category of property that *cannot* be transferred by will are properties that have a designated beneficiary outside of the provisions of your will. In general, if there is already a valid determination of who will receive the property upon your death (as there is, for example, in the choice of a life insurance beneficiary), you may not alter this choice of beneficiary through the use of your will. If you wish to alter your choice of beneficiary in any of these cases, please alter the choice directly with the holder of the particular property (for instance, the life insurance company or bank). These types of properties include:
- Life insurance policies
- Retirement plans
- IRAs and KEOGHs
- Pension plans
- Trust bank accounts
- Living trust assets
- Payable-on-death bank accounts
- U.S. Savings Bonds, with payable-on-death beneficiaries

The next category of property that may have certain restrictions regarding its transfer by will is property of which you may own only a certain share or percentage. Examples of this may be a partnership interest in a company or a jointly-held property. Using a will, you may leave only that percentage or fraction of the ownership of the property that is actually yours.

The ownership rights and shares of property owned jointly must be considered. Several states, mostly in the western United States, follow the *community property* type of marital property system. The community property states are: Alaska (by written agreement between the spouses), Arizona, California, Idaho, Louisiana, Nevada, New Mexico, Texas, Washington, and Wisconsin. All property owned by either spouse during a marriage is divided into two types: separate property and community property. *Separate property* consists of all property considered to be owned entirely by one spouse. Separate property, essentially, is all property owned by the spouse prior to the marriage and kept separate during the marriage, and all property received individually by the spouse by gift or inheritance during the marriage. All other property is considered *community property*. In other words, all property acquired during the marriage by either spouse, unless by gift or inheritance, is community property. Community property is considered to be owned in equal shares by each spouse, regardless of whose efforts actually went into acquiring the property. *Note*: Alaska allows spouses to create community property by mutual agreement. (One major exception to this general rule are Social Security and railroad retirement benefits, which are considered to be separate property by Federal law). Thus, if you are a married resident of a community property state, the property that you may dispose of by will consists of all of your separate property and one-half of your jointly owned marital community property. The other half of the community property automatically becomes your spouse's sole property upon your death. Residents of community property states may also own property jointly as *tenants-in-common* or as *joint tenants*. Residents of all other states are governed by a *common-law property* system. Under this system, there is no rule that gives 50 percent ownership of the property acquired during marriage to each spouse. In common-law states, the property that you may dispose of with your will consists of all the property held by title in your name, any property that you have earned or purchased with your own money, and any property that you may have been given as a gift or inherited, either before or after your marriage.

If your name alone is on a title document (for instance, a deed or automobile title) in common-law states, then you own it solely. If your name and your spouse's name are both on the document, you generally own it as tenants-in-common, unless the document specifically states that your ownership is to be as joint tenants or, if your state allows, as a *tenancy-by-the-entireties* (a form of joint tenancy between married persons). There is an important difference between these types of joint ownership: namely, survivorship. With property owned as tenants-in-common, the percentage or fraction that each tenant-in-common owns is property that may be disposed of under a will. If the property is held as joint tenants or as tenants-by-the entireties, the survivor automatically receives the deceased party's share. Thus, in your will, you may not dispose of any property held in joint tenancy or tenancy-by-the entirety since it already has an automatic legal disposition upon your death. If you are married however, there is a further restriction on your right to dispose of property by will. All common-law states protect spouses from total disinheritance by providing a statutory scheme under which a spouse may choose to take a minimum share of the deceased spouse's estate, regardless of what the will states. This effectively prevents any spouse from being entirely disinherited through the use of the common-law rules of property (in other words, name on the title = ownership of the property).

Regardless of which type of state that you live in (community property or common law), once you have determined which of your property is able to be gifted to others using your will, you should make a list of your property in preparation for the next important decisions regarding who will receive your property upon your death. For this purpose, you may wish to use that Property Questionnaire that is included on the CD as a PDF file

Beneficiary Instructions

Any person or organization who receives property under a will is termed a *beneficiary* of that will. Any person or organization can receive property under a will unless the beneficiary falls into certain narrow categories of disqualification. Those who can receive property as beneficiaries include any family members, the named executor, any illegitimate children (if named specifically), corporations, charities (but see below for possible restrictions), creditors, debtors, and any friends, acquaintances, or even strangers. The few categories of disqualified beneficiaries are as follows:

- An attorney who drafts the will is generally assumed to have used undue influence if he or she is made a beneficiary
- Many states disqualify any witnesses to the execution of the will. However, to be safe, it is recommended that none of your witnesses be beneficiaries under your will
- A person who murders someone is universally disqualified from receiving any property under the murdered person's will
- An unincorporated association is typically not allowed to receive property under a will. This particular disqualification stems from the fact that such associations generally have no legal right to hold property
- A few states also have restrictions on the right to leave property to charitable organizations and churches. If you intend to leave large sums of money or property to a charitable organization or church, please check with a competent attorney.

You are advised to review your will periodically and make any necessary changes as your marital or family situation may dictate. If you are divorced, married, remarried, widowed, or adopt or have a child, there may be unforeseen consequences based on the way you have written your will. Each state has differing laws on the effect of marriage and divorce on a person's will. Your will should be prepared with regard to how your life is presently arranged. Your will should, however, always be reviewed and updated each time there is a substantial change in your life. Once you have identified the persons (or organizations) that you would like to receive your property upon your death, you should make a list of the designated beneficiaries and the property that you would like them to receive. For this purpose, you may wish to use the Beneficiary Questionnaire that is included on the CD as a PDF file. As will be explained in the next section, the will forms provided in this book are set up to allow you to choose 'alternative beneficiaries,' that is a person chosen to receive the property in the event that the chosen beneficiary is deceased or declines your gift.

Preparing Your Will

At the back of this book (and on the CD), you will find two separate wills that have been prepared for the purpose of allowing persons whose situations fall into certain standard formats to prepare their wills quickly and easily on pre-assembled forms. Generally, the wills are for a person with children and for a person without children. Please read the description of each will later in this section to be certain that the will you choose is appropriate for your particular situation. Also note that each of the wills in this book is intended to be a *self-proving* will. This means that the signatures of the witnesses and the testator will be verified by a notary public and thus, the witnesses' testimony will not be needed in probate court at a later date in order to authenticate their signatures. These pre-assembled will forms are intended to be used as simplified worksheets for preparing your own personal will. The forms should be filled-in by hand and then retyped according to the instructions. These pre-assembled wills are not intended to be filled in and used "as is" as an original will. Such use would most likely result in an invalid will. Be certain to carefully follow all of the instructions for use of these forms. The forms are not difficult to fill out, but must be prepared properly in order to be legally valid. To prepare either of the wills in this book, you should follow these simple steps:

① Carefully read through the will form to determine if the clauses provided are suitable for your situation. Choose the will that is most appropriate. Print out or make a photocopy of the will that you select to use as a worksheet. If you wish, you may use the form in the book itself as a worksheet. Using your lists of beneficiaries and property to be gifted to each of them, fill in the appropriate clauses on your worksheet version of your will.

② After you have filled in all of the appropriate information, carefully reread your entire will. Be certain that it contains all of the correct information that you desire. Then, starting at the beginning of the will, cross out all of the words and phrases in the worksheet will form that do not apply in your situation.

③ When you have completed all of your will clauses, turn to page 16 for instructions on the typing and final preparation of your will.

As you fill in the information for each clause, keep in mind the following instructions:

Title Clause: The title clause is mandatory for all wills and must be included. Fill in the name blank with your full legal name. If you have been known by more than one name, use your principal name.

Identification Clause: The identification clause is mandatory and must be included in all wills. In the first blank, include any other names that you are known by. Do this by adding the phrase: "also known as" after your principal full name. For example:

John James Smith, also known as Jimmy John Smith.

In the spaces provided for your residence, use the location of your principal residence; that is, the place where you currently live permanently.

Marital Status Clause: Each of the pre-assembled will forms in this book may be used by either a married or single person. Select the proper will and fill in the appropriate description of your marital status information (you may use more than one clause, if appropriate), such as: [My marital status is that:]:

> I am currently married to [_name of your current spouse_].

> I have never been married.

> I was previously married to [_name of your former spouse_], and that marriage ended by [_select either_ death, divorce, or annulment].

Identification of Children Clause: This clause is only be present in the pre-assembled will for people with children. In this clause, you should specifically identify all of your children, indicating their full names, current addresses, and dates of birth.

Identification of Grandchildren Clause: This clause is only be used in the pre-assembled will for people with children. If you do not have grandchildren, cross out this entire clause. If you do have grandchildren, you should specifically identify all of your grandchildren in this clause, indicating their full names, current addresses, and dates of birth.

Specific Gifts Clause: For making specific gifts, use as many of the "I give ..." paragraphs as is necessary to complete your chosen gifts. In these paragraphs, you may make any type of gift that you wish; either a cash gift, a gift of a specific piece of personal property or real estate, or a specific share of your total estate. If you wish to give some of your estate in the form of portions of the total, it is recommended to use fractional portions. For example, if you wish to leave your estate in equal shares to two persons, use "I give one-half of my total estate to..." for each party. Although neither of the wills in this book contain a specific clause that states that you give one person your entire estate, you may make such a gift using this clause by simply stating:

> "I give my entire estate to...."

Be sure that you do not attempt to give any other gifts. However, you should still include the *residuary clause* in your will, which is explained below.

In your description of the property, you should be as specific and precise as possible. For land, it is suggested that you use the description exactly as shown on the deed to the property. For personal property, be certain that your description clearly differentiates your gift from any other property. For example: "I give my blue velvet coat which was a gift from my brother John to...." Use serial numbers, colors, or any other descriptive words to clearly indicate the exact nature of the gift. For cash gifts, specifically indicate the amount of the gift. For gifts of securities, state the amount of shares and the name of the company. You may add simple conditions to the gifts that you make, if you desire. For example, you may state "I give $1,000.00 to the Centerville Church for use in purchasing a new roof for the church." Complex conditions, however, are not possible in this clause, and immoral or illegal conditions are not acceptable. Be sure to clearly identify the beneficiary and alternate beneficiary by their full names. You can also name joint beneficiaries, such as several children, if you choose. The space provided for an identification of the relationship of the beneficiary can simply be a descriptive phrase like "my wife," "my brother-in-law," or "my best friend." It does not mean that the beneficiary must be related to you personally.

The choice of alternate beneficiary is for the purpose of allowing you to designate someone else to receive the gift if your first choice to receive the gift dies before you do (or, in the case of a organization chosen as primary beneficiary, is no longer in business). In this or any of the other gift clauses, your choice for alternate beneficiary may be one or more persons or an organization. It is recommended to always specifically name your beneficiary(ies), rather than using a description only, such as "my children." In addition, you may delete the alternate beneficiary choice and substitute the words "the residue" instead. The *residue* is all property remaining in your estate after all expenses, taxes, and gifts have been paid. The result of this change will be that if your primary beneficiary dies before you do, your gift will pass under your residuary clause, which is discussed below. If additional gifts are desired, simply print out or photocopy an additional page to use as a worksheet.

Residuary Clause: Although not a technical legal requirement, it is strongly recommended that you include the residuary clause in every will. With this clause, you will choose the person(s) or organization(s) to receive anything that is not covered by other clauses of your will. If, for any reason, any other gifts under your will are not able to be completed, this clause goes into effect. For example, if a beneficiary refuses to accept your gift, the chosen beneficiary has died and no alternate was selected, or both the beneficiary and alternate has died, the gift is put back into your estate and would *pass under* (be distributed under the terms of) the residuary clause. If there is no residuary clause included in your will, any property not disposed of under your will is treated as though you did not have a will and could potentially be forfeited to the state. To avoid this, it is strongly recommended that you make this clause mandatory in your will. In addition, you may use this clause to give all of your estate (except your specific gifts) to one or more persons. For example: you make specific gifts of $1,000.00 to a sister and a car to a friend. By then naming your spouse as the residuary clause beneficiary, you will have gifted everything in your estate to your spouse—except the $1,000.00 and the car. You could then name your children, in equal shares, as the alternate residuary beneficiaries. In this manner, if your spouse were to die first, your children would then equally share your entire estate—except the $1,000.00 and the car.

Be sure to clearly identify the beneficiary by full name. The space provided for an identification of the relationship of the beneficiary can simply be a descriptive phrase like "my wife," "my brother-in-law," or "my best friend." It does not mean that the beneficiary must be related to you personally.

Survivorship Clause: This clause is included in every will. This clause provides for two possibilities. First, it provides for a required period of survival for any beneficiary, in order to receive a gift under your will. The practical effect of this is to be certain that your property passes under your will and not under that of a beneficiary who dies shortly after receiving your gift. The second portion of this clause provides for a determination of how your property should pass in the eventuality that both you and a beneficiary (most likely your spouse) should die in a manner that makes it impossible to determine who died first. Without this clause in your will, it would be possible that property could momentarily pass to a beneficiary under your will. When that person dies (possibly immediately, if a result of a common accident or disaster), your property could wind up being left to the person whom your beneficiary designated, rather than to your alternate beneficiary. If you and your spouse are both preparing wills, it is a good idea to be certain that each of your wills contains identical survivorship clauses. If you are each other's primary beneficiary, it is also wise to attempt to coordinate who your alternate beneficiaries may be in the event of simultaneous deaths of you and your spouse.

Executor Clause: The executor clause must be included in every will. With this clause, you will make your choice of *executor*, the person who will administer and distribute your estate, and an alternate choice if your first choice is unable to serve. A spouse, sibling, or other trusted party is usually chosen to act as executor. The person chosen should be a resident of the state in which you currently reside. Note that you allow your executor to seek independent administration of your estate. Where allowed by state law, this enables your executor to manage your estate with minimal court supervision and can save your estate extensive court costs and legal fees. Additionally, you grant the executor broad powers to manage your estate and also provide that he or she not be required to post a bond in order to be appointed to serve as executor. Be sure to clearly identify the executor and alternate executor by their full names. The space provided for an identification of the relationship of the executor can simply be a descriptive phrase like "my wife," "my brother-in-law," or "my best friend." It does not mean that the executor must be related to you personally.

Child Guardianship Clause: This clause will only be present in the pre-assembled will that relates to children. With this clause, you may designate your choice as to whom you wish to care for any of your minor children after you are gone. If none of your children are minors, you may delete this clause. Who you choose to be the guardian of your children is an important matter. If you are married, your spouse is generally appointed by the probate or family court, regardless of your designation in a will. However, even if you are married, it is a good idea to choose your spouse as first choice and then provide a second choice. This will cover the contingency in which both you and your spouse die in a single accident. Your choice should obviously be a trusted person whom you feel would provide the best care for your children in your absence. Be aware, however, that the court is guided, but not bound, by this particular choice in your will. The court's decision in appointing a child's guardian is based upon what would be in the best interests of the child. In most situations, however, a parent's choice as to who should be his or her child's guardian is almost universally followed by the courts. Additionally, you grant the guardian broad power to care for and manage your children's property and also provide that the appointed guardian not be required to post a bond in order to be appointed. Be sure to clearly identify the guardian and alternate guardian by full name. The space provided for an identification of the relationship of the guardian can simply be a descriptive phrase like "my wife," "my brother-in-law," or "my best friend." It does not mean that the guardian must be related to you personally.

Children's Trust Fund Clause: This clause will only be present in the pre-assembled will that relates to children. It is by using this clause that you may set up a trust fund for any gifts you have made to your minor children. You also may delay the time when they will actually have unrestricted control over your gift. It is not recommended, however, to attempt to delay receipt of control beyond the age of 30. If you have left assets to more than one child, this clause provides that individual trusts be set up for each child. If none of your children are minors, you may delete this clause. The choice for trustee under a children's trust should generally be the same person whom you have chosen to be the children's guardian. This is not, however, a requirement. The choice of trustee is generally a spouse if alive, with the alternate being a trusted friend or family member. Be sure to clearly identify the trustee and alternate trustee by full name. The space provided for an identification of the relationship of the trustee can simply be a descriptive phrase like "my wife," "my brother-in-law," or "my best friend." It does not mean that the trustee must be related to you personally. The terms of the trust provide that the trustee may distribute any or all of the income or principal to the children as the trustee deems necessary to provide for the children's health, support, and education. The trust will terminate when either the child's specific age is reached, all of the money is spent prior to that age, or the child dies prematurely. Upon termination, any remaining trust funds will be distributed to the child (beneficiary) if surviving; if not surviving, to the heirs of the beneficiary (if any); or if there are no heirs of the beneficiary, to the residue of your estate. Additionally, you grant the trustee broad power to manage the trust and also provide that he or she not be required to post a bond in order to be appointed.

Organ Donation Clause: The use of this clause is optional. If you choose not to use this clause, you may delete it from your will. Use this clause to provide for any use of your body after death. You may, if you so desire, limit your donation to certain parts; for example, only your eyes. If so desired, simply delete "any of my body parts and/or organs" from the following provision and insert your chosen donation. A copy of your will or instructions regarding this donation should be kept in a place that is readily accessible by your executor and spouse.

Funeral Arrangements Clause: The use of this clause is optional. If you choose not to use this clause, you may delete it from your will. Use this clause to make known your wishes as to funeral and burial arrangements. Since it may be difficult to obtain your will quickly in an emergency, it is also a good idea to leave information regarding these desires with your executor, your spouse, a close friend, or a relative.

Signature and Self-Proving Clause: The signature lines and final paragraph of this clause must be included in your will. You will fill in the number of pages and the appropriate dates where indicated after you have properly typed your will or had it typed. The use of the notary acknowledgment, although not a strict legal necessity, is strongly recommended. This allows the will to become "self-proving" and the witnesses need not be called upon to testify in court at a later date after your death that they, indeed, signed the will as witnesses. Although a few states have not enacted legislation to allow for the use of this type of sworn and acknowledged testimony to be used in court, the current trend is to allow for its use in probate courts. This saves time, money, and trouble in having your will admitted to *probate* (the court administration of your will) when necessary. The actual signing of the will by both you and your witnesses will be explained later in this section, following the description of the will forms.

Will for a Person with Children (Using Children's Trust)

This will form is appropriate for use by a person with one or more children. There are also provisions in this will for use if the parent has minor children and desires to place the property and assets that may be left to the children into a trust fund. In addition, this will allows a parent to choose a person to act as guardian for any minor children. In most cases, a married person may desire to choose the other spouse as both trustee and guardian for any of their children, although this is not a legal requirement. If the parent has no *minor* children, the will clauses relating to the children's trust and to guardianship of the children may be deleted. Each spouse/parent must prepare his or her own will. Do not attempt to prepare a joint will for both you and your spouse together.

Will for a Person with No Children

This will form is appropriate for use by a person with no children or grandchildren. If you are married, each spouse must prepare his or her own will. Do not attempt to prepare a joint will for both you and your spouse together.

Completing and Signing Your Will

Using your 'worksheet' version of your will, print out or type your entire will on clean white sheets of 8½" x 11" paper. Make sure that there are no corrections or erasures on the final copy. Do not attempt to correct the mistakes on the final copy. If you make a mistake, reprint or retype that particular page. After you have prepared your will in the proper form (either retyped or on your computer), you are ready to sign it. *Do not* sign your will however, until you have read this section and have all of the necessary witnesses and notary public present. The legal requirements listed in this section regarding the proper *execution* (signing) of your will are extremely important and must not be deviated from in any manner in order for your will to be legally valid. These requirements are not at all difficult to follow, but they must be followed precisely. These formal requirements are what transform your will from a mere piece of paper outlining your wishes into a legal document that grants the power to dispose of your property under court order after your death. The reasons for the formality of these requirements are twofold: first, by requiring a ceremonial-type signing of the document, it is hoped that the testator is made fully aware of the importance of what he or she is doing; and second, by requiring a formal signing witnessed by other adults, it is hoped that any instances of forgery, fraud, and coercion will be avoided, or at least minimized. Again, these legal formalities must be observed strictly. *Do not* deviate from these instructions in any way. The formal execution or signing of your will makes it legally valid and failure to properly sign your will renders it invalid. To properly execute your will, follow these few simple steps:

① Select three witnesses who will be available to assist you in witnessing your will. These persons may be any adults who are not mentioned in the will either as a beneficiary, executor, trustee, or guardian. The witnesses can be friends, neighbors, co-workers, or even strangers. However, it is prudent to choose persons who have been stable members of your community, since they may be called upon to testify in court someday.

② Arrange for all of your witnesses to meet you at the office or home of a local notary public. Many banks, real estate offices, and government offices have notary services and most will be glad to assist you. (The notary public may *not* be one of the required three witnesses.)
③ In front of all of the witnesses and the notary public, the following should take place in the order shown:

(a) You should state: "This is my Last Will and Testament, which I am about to sign. I ask that each of you witness my signature." There is no requirement that the witnesses know any of the terms of your will or that they read any of your will. All that is necessary is that they hear you state that it is your will, that you request them to be witnesses, that they observe you sign your will, and that they also sign the will as witnesses in each other's presence.

(b) You will then sign your will in ink, using a pen, at the end of the will in the place indicated, exactly as your name is printed or typed on your will. You should also sign your initials on the bottom of each page of your will at this time.

(c) After you have signed, pass your will to the first witness, who should sign in the place indicated and fill in his or her address.

(d) After the first witness has signed, have the will passed to the second witness, who should also sign in the place indicated and fill in his or her address.

(e) After the second witness has signed, have the will passed to the third and final witness, who also signs in the place indicated and fills in his or her address. Throughout this ceremony, you and all of the witnesses must remain together. It is easier if you are all seated around a table or desk.

(f) For the final step, the notary public completes the notary acknowledgment section of the will and signs in the space indicated. When this step is completed, your will is a valid legal document and you can be assured that your wishes will be carried out upon the presentation of your will to a probate court upon your death.

Please note that you should *never* under any circumstances sign a duplicate of your will. Once your will has been properly executed following the steps above, you may make photocopies of it. It is a good idea to clearly label any of these photocopies as "COPIES."

Having completed your will according to the instructions above, it is now time to place your will in a safe place. Many people keep their important papers in a safe deposit box at a local bank. Although this is an acceptable place for storing a will, be advised that there are certain drawbacks. Your will should be in a place that is readily accessible at a moment's notice to your executor. Often there are certain unavoidable delays in gaining access to a safe deposit box in an emergency situation. If you are married, and your safe deposit box is jointly held, many of these delays can be avoided. However, even in this situation, some states prevent immediate access to the safe deposit box of a deceased married person. If you decide to keep the original will in your safe deposit box, it is a good idea to keep a copy of your will clearly marked "COPY" at home in a safe but easily-located place, with a note as to where the original will can be found. An acceptable alternative to a safe deposit box is a home file box or desk that is used for home storage of your important papers. If possible, this storage place should be fireproof and under lock and key.

Wherever you decide to store your will, you will need to inform your chosen executor of its location. The executor will need to obtain the original of your will shortly after your demise to determine if there are any necessary duties that must be looked after without delay; for example, funeral plans or organ donations. It is also a good practice to store any life insurance policies and a copy of your birth certificate in the same location as your original will. Any title documents or deeds relating to property that will be transferred under your will may also be stored with your will for the convenience of your executor. One final precaution: If you allow your executor to keep a copy of your will, be certain that you immediately inform him or her of any new will that you prepare, of any *codicils* (formal changes to your will) you make to your will, or of any decision to *revoke* (cancel) your will.

Living Wills

A *living will* is a relatively new legal document which has been made necessary by the advent of recent technological advances in the field of medicine that can allow for the continued existence of a person on advanced life-support systems long after any normal semblance of "life," as many people consider it, has ceased. The inherent problem that is raised by this type of extraordinary medical "life-support" is that the person whose life is being artificially continued by such means may not wish to be kept alive beyond what he or she may consider to be the proper time for his or her life to end. However, since a person in such condition has no method of communicating his or her wishes to the medical or legal authorities in charge, a living will was developed which allows one to make these important decisions in advance of the situation. As more and more advances are made in the medical field in terms of the ability to prevent "clinical" death, the difficult situations envisioned by a living will are destined to occur more often. The legal acceptance of a living will is currently at the forefront of new laws being added in many states. Although this living will does not address all possible contingencies regarding terminally ill patients, it does provide a written declaration for the individual to make known his or her or decisions on life-prolonging procedures. A living will declares your wishes not to be kept alive by artificial or mechanical means if you are suffering from a terminal condition and your death would be imminent without the use of such artificial means. A living will provides a legally binding written set of instructions regarding your wishes about this important matter. Note that a living will is also included in the Advance Health Care Directive in this kit and discussed later.

In order to qualify for the use of a living will, you must meet the following basic criteria:

- You must be at least 19 years of age
- You must be of "sound mind" and able to comprehend the nature of your action in signing such a document

If you desire that your life not be prolonged artificially when there is no reasonable chance for recovery and death is imminent, please follow the instructions for completion of your living will. Healthcare professionals and physicians will be guided by this expression of your desires concerning life-support.

Preparing and Signing a Living Will

① Make a photocopy or print out a copy of the entire living will form from this book or CD. Using the copy, please fill in the correct information in the appropriate blanks. On clean, white, 8½" x 11" paper, type or print out the entire living will exactly as shown with your information added. Carefully re-read this original living will to be certain that it expresses your desires exactly on this very important matter. When you have a clean, clear original typed or printed version, staple all of the pages together in the upper left-hand corner. *Do not* yet sign this document or fill in the date.

② You should now assemble three witnesses and a notary public to witness your signature. As noted on the document itself, these witnesses should have no connection with you from a healthcare or beneficiary standpoint. Specifically, the witnesses must:
- Be at least 19 years of age
- Not be related to you in any manner: by blood, marriage, or adoption
- Not be your attending physician, or a patient or employee of your attending physician; or a patient, physician, or employee of the healthcare facility in which you may be a patient. However, please see the paragraph below
- Not be entitled to any portion of your estate upon your death under any laws of intestate succession, under your will, or under any codicil

- Have no claim against any portion of your estate upon your death
- Not be directly responsible financially for your medical care
- Not have signed the living will *for* you, even at your direction
- Not be paid a fee for acting as a witness

In addition, please note that several states and the District of Columbia have laws in effect regarding witnesses when the declarant is a patient in a nursing home, boarding facility, hospital, or skilled or intermediate healthcare facility. In those situations, it is advisable to have a patient ombudsman, patient advocate, or the director of the healthcare facility to act as the third witness to the signing of a living will. If you are a resident of a healthcare facility, please ask the facility's legal advisor for the correct procedure.

③ In front of all of the witnesses and the notary public, the following should take place in the order shown:

- You should state: "This is my Living Will which I am about to sign. I ask that each of you witness my signature." There is no requirement that the witnesses know any of the terms of your living will or that they read any of your living will. All that is necessary is that they hear you state that it is your living will, that you request them to be witnesses, that they observe you sign your living will, and that they also sign the living will as witnesses in each other's presence.

- You will then sign your living will exactly as your name is printed, at the end of your living will, where indicated, in ink using a pen. After you have signed, pass your living will to the first witness, who should sign where indicated and fill in his or her address.

- After the first witness has signed, have the living will passed to the second witness, who should also sign where indicated. After the second witness has signed, have the living will passed to the third and final witness, who also signs where indicated and fills in his or her address. Throughout this ceremony, you and all of the witnesses must remain together.

- The final step is for the notary public to sign in the space indicated. When this step is completed, your living will is a valid legal document. Have several copies made and, if appropriate, deliver a copy to your attending physician to have placed in your medical records file. You may also desire to give copies to the person you have chosen as the executor of your will, to your clergy, and to your spouse or other trusted relative.

Note: If you are at all unsure of the correct use of the living will form in this section, please first check your state's lising in the Appendix on Estate Planning Laws and also, if necessary, please consult a competent attorney.

Instructions for Revocation of Your Living Will

All states that have recognized living wills have provided methods for the easy revocation of them. Since a living will provides authority to medical personnel to withhold life-support technology which will likely result in death to the patient, great care must be taken to insure that a change of mind by the patient is heeded. For the revocation of a living will, any one of the following methods of revocation is generally acceptable:

- Physical destruction of the living will, such as tearing, burning, or mutilating the document

- A written revocation of the living will by you or by a person acting at your direction. A form for this is provided as a tear-out and on the CD. You may use two witnesses on this form, although most states do not require the use of witnesses for the written revocation of a living will to be valid

- An oral revocation in the presence of a witness who signs and dates a document confirming a revocation. This oral declaration may take any form. Most states allow for a person to revoke such a document by any indication (even non-verbal) of his or her intent to revoke a living will, regardless of his or her physical or mental condition

To use the Revocation of Living Will, print out or photocopy the form from the book or CD. Fill in the appropriate information, print or retype the form, and sign it. In addition, your two witnesses may sign it at the same time.

Advance Health Care Directives

An Advance Health Care Directive is a legal document that may be used in any state that allows you to provide written directions relating to your future health care should you become incapacitated and unable to speak for yourself. Advance Health Care Directives give you a direct voice in medical decisions in situations when you cannot make those decisions yourself. Your Advance Health Care Directive will not be used as long as you are able to express your own decisions. You can always accept or refuse medical treatment and you always have the legal right to revoke your Advance Health Care Directive at any time. The Federal Patient Self-Determination Act encourages all people to make their own decisions about the type of medical care they wish to receive. This act also requires all health care agencies (hospitals, long-term care facilities, and home health agencies) receiving Medicare and Medicaid reimbursement to recognize a living will and health care power of attorney as advance directives. Under this Act, all health care agencies must ask you if you have advance directives and must give you materials with information about your rights under state law.

Advance Health Care Directives are not only for senior citizens. Serious life-threatening accidents or disease can strike anyone and leave them unable to communicate their desires. In fact, the rise of the use of Advance Health Care Directives can be attributed in part, to legal cases involving medical care to young people, particularly Karen Ann Quinlan and Nancy Cruzan, and most recently, Terry Schiavo. Anyone over the age of 18 who is mentally competent should complete an Advance Health Care Directive. Be aware, however, that Advance Health Care Directives are intended for non-emergency medical treatment. Most often, there is no time for health care providers to consult and analyze the provisions of an Advance Health Care Directive in an emergency situation.

The Advance Health Care Directives that are provided on the CD contain four separate sections, each dealing with different aspects of potential situations that may arise during a possible period of incapacitation:

- Living Will
- Selection of Health Care Agent (generally, by Health Care Power of Attorney)
- Designation of Primary Physician
- Organ Donation

In addition, this book also provides a two other legal forms that may be useful in many health care situations if you are unable to handle your own financial affairs: Durable Powers of Attorney for Financial Affairs (either effective immediately or effective only upon your disability). Please see page 8 for explanations of each of these legal forms.

The state-specific Advance Health Care Directive forms in this kit are only provided on the CD. Should you choose to use this type of form, you need not necessarily adopt all four sections of the document for your own use. You may select and complete any or all of the four separate sections of the form. Many people find using a state-specific document easier than completing each separate form as an individual document. This method also provides a simple compact package that contains your entire Advance Health Care Directive with forms using legal language that most health care providers in your state are familiar with. In a few states, the legislatures have not developed specific language for one or more of the forms. In such situations, an appropriate and legally-valid form has been added to the directives for those states. Any such forms have been prepared legal professionals following any guidelines set out by the state's legislature. Before continuing, please check your state's listing in the Estate Planning Appendix on the CD.

Preparing and Signing Your Advance Health Care Directive

① Select the appropriate form for your state on the Forms-on-CD. Carefully read through each section of your Advance Health Care Directive. You may wish to make two copies of the form(s) that you choose. This will allow you to use one form as a draft copy and the other form for a final copy that you, your witnesses, and a notary will sign.

② You will need to initial your choices in the first section of the form as to which sections of the entire Advance Health Care Directive you wish to be effective. The choices are:

- Living Will
- Selection of Health Care Agent
- Designation of Primary Physician
- Organ Donation

If you do not wish to use a particular main section of the entire form, cross out that section of the form clearly and do not initial that section in either the first paragraph of the Directive or in the paragraph directly before your signature near the end of the Directive. If you do not wish to use a particular paragraph within one of the four main sections of the form, cross out that paragraph also.

③ For all forms, make the appropriate choices in each section where indicated by initialing the designated place or filling in the appropriate information. Depending on which form that you use, you may have many choices to initial or you may have no choices to initial. Please carefully read through the paragraphs and clauses that require choices to be certain that you understand the choices that you will be making. If you wish to add additional instructions or limitations in the places indicated on the form, please type or clearly print your instructions. If you need to add additional pages, please use the form titled "Additional Information for Advance Health Care Directive" which is also provided on the CD. If you need and use additional pages, be certain that you initial and date each added page and that you clearly label each additional page regarding which paragraph or section of the form to which it pertains.

④ In the section on Organ Donations, you may choose to either donate all of your organs or limit your donation to certain specific organs. Likewise, you may provide that the organs be used for any purpose or you may limit their use to certain purposes.

⑤ Finally, you will need to complete the signature and witness/notary sections of your forms. When you have a completed original with no erasures or corrections, staple all of the pages together in the upper left-hand corner. Do not sign this document or fill in the date yet. You should now assemble your witnesses and a notary public to witness your signature. Be certain that your witnesses meet your specific state requirements as noted in the witness section. In addition, please note that several states and the District of Columbia have laws in effect regarding witnesses when the declarant is a patient in a nursing home, boarding facility, hospital, or skilled or intermediate health care facility. In those situations, it is advisable to have a patient ombudsman, patient advocate, or the director of the health care facility to act as the third witness to the signing of an Advance Health Care Directive. In order that your Advance Health Care Directive be accepted by all legal and medical authorities with as little difficulty as possible, it is highly recommended that you have your signing of this important document witnessed by both your appropriate witnesses and a notary public.

⑥ In front of all of the witnesses and the notary public, the following should take place in the order shown:

(a) There is no requirement that the witnesses know any of the terms of your Advance Health Care Directive or other legal forms, or that they read any of your Advance Health Care Directive. All that is necessary is that they observe you sign your Advance Health Care Directive and that they also sign the Advance Health Care Directive as witnesses in each other's presence.

(b) You will sign your form at the end where indicated, exactly as your name is written on the form, in ink using a pen. At this time, you should also again initial your choices as to which sections you have chosen (directly before your signature space). You will also need to fill in the date on the first page of the Directive, date and initial each Additional Information Page (if you have used any), and fill in your address after your signature. Once you have signed and completed all of the necessary information, pass your Advance Health Care Directive or other legal form to the first witness, who should sign and date the acknowledgment where indicated and also print his or her name.

(c) After the first witness has signed, have the Advance Health Care Directive or other legal form passed to the second and then third witness, who should both also sign and date the acknowledgment where indicated and print his or her name.

(d) Throughout this ceremony, you and all of the witnesses must remain together. The final step is for the notary public to sign in the space where indicated and complete the notarization block on the form.

(e) If you have chosen individuals to act as either your Health Care Agent (Durable Power of Attorney for Health Care), you should have them sign the form at the end where shown acknowledging that they accept their appointment.

⑦ When this step is completed, your Advance Health Care Directive that you have signed is a valid legal document. Have several photo-copies made and, if appropriate, deliver a copy to your attending physician or health care facility to have placed in your medical records file. You should also provide a copy to any person who was selected as either your Health Care Agent or your Agent for Financial Affairs. You may also desire to give a copy to the person you have chosen as the executor of your will, your clergy, and your spouse or other trusted relative. Finally, a Revocaton of Advance Health Care Directive is included only on the Forms-on-CD.

Living Trusts

A *living trust* or revocable trust is a legal document that is used to pass on your assets to your beneficiaries upon your death. Thus, it accomplishes much the same results as a will. Like a will, it is revocable at any time during your life. Also, like a will, it allows you to retain control over your assets during your life and affords no direct tax advantages. However, it does have a few advantages over a will and a few disadvantages, as well. The main advantage to using a living trust instead of a will is that it allows your assets to be passed to your beneficiaries automatically upon your death, without any delay, probate, court intervention, or lawyer's fees. To many people, this very important advantage outweighs any disadvantages. Another advantage is that it is much more difficult to challenge a living trust in court than it is to challenge a will. Finally, a living trust is a more private document that only needs to be recorded with the county recorder in the event that real estate is transferred with such a trust. Perhaps the most important disadvantage of using a living trust is the need to actually transfer to the trust all of the property intended to be put in trust. This requirement and the need to keep accurate trust records make the actual mechanics of a living trust more complicated than simply preparing a will.

Even if you decide to use a living trust to pass your assets to your beneficiaries, you will also need to prepare a will. This is because regardless of your best efforts, generally, you will not be able to name each and every item of property that you own. Without a will as a backup, any property not named in the living trust will pass to your closest relatives, or if there are none, the property may be forfeited to the state.

To create a living trust, you will first need to decide what property you wish to place in trust. To do this, you may wish to review the property information in the *Wills* section previously noted and you may use the Property Questionnaire that is included on the CD for this purpose. Assets that are subject to being sold or discarded regularly should not be put in the trust. Next, you will need to decide who is to receive your assets upon your death. Again, you may wish to review the beneficiary information included previously under the *Wills* section, and, again you may wish to use the Beneficiary Questionnaire that is included on the CD.

Finally, you will need to decide if you wish to retain all control over the trust. To achieve this end, you will name yourself as trustee. Once you have created your living trust, you will need to actually transfer the ownership of all of the assets selected to the trust. This transfer may include obtaining a new title to your car, new bank accounts, and a new deed to any real estate. The new ownership will be in the name of the trust itself, with the name of the trustee specified; for example, *The Jane Smith Revocable Living Trust; Jane Smith, Trustee* might be the name on the deed or title. *Note*: In order to transfer property into your trust, you may need to use an Assignment to Living Trust form for personal property (see below) or a Quitclaim Deed for real estate (see below under Sale of Real Estate forms). (NY Residents must file a Notice of Assignment with their local court clerk).

Note: Some states require registration of Living Trusts. Be check your state's listing in the Estate Planning Appendix and, if necessary, use the Registration of Living Trust form on the CD. *Note*: If you are at all unsure of the correct use of these forms, please consult a competent attorney.

Living Trust: Needed for this form is the following information: the name and address of the *grantor* (the one who is creating the trust), the date the trust will take effect, the name of the *trustee* (the one who will have control over the trust, usually the same person as the grantor), the marital status of the grantor, the name of a successor trustee (usually a spouse, child of legal age, or trusted friend), the name of the state in which you reside, and the signature of the grantor/trustee. The signature on this form should be notarized. This form of trust reserves the right to allow you to cancel or amend this trust at any time.

Schedule of Assets of Living Trust: On this form, you will include a listing of all of the property that you wish to transfer into the trust. This document should be attached to the living trust when completed. This form needs to be notarized.

Schedule of Beneficiaries of Living Trust: On this form, you will include a list of all of your chosen beneficiaries, alternate beneficiaries, and the trust property that you wish them to receive. You will also choose a residual beneficiary. (For more information on beneficiary choices, refer to the section on Wills). This form must be notarized.

Assignment to Living Trust: This form is used to transfer personal property to the trust. Provide a full description of the property transferred. This form should also be notarized.

Amendment of Living Trust: This form is used to make any changes to the living trust; for example, adding or deleting any of the property listed on the Schedule of Assets or changing a beneficiary on the Schedule of Beneficiaries of Living Trust. Simply fill in the name and address of the grantor/trustee and specify the changes to the trust. The signature on this document should also be notarized.

Revocation of Living Trust: This document is used whenever you desire to terminate the trust. You may do this at any time. To revoke your trust, simply fill in the name and address of the grantor/trustee and the date of the original trust. The signature on this document should also be notarized.

Releases

A release is a method of acknowledging the satisfaction of an obligation or of releasing parties from liability or claims. Releases are used in various situations: from releasing a person or company from liability after an accident, to a release of liens or claims against property. They can be a useful means of settling minor disputes. One party may pay another to release a claim. For example: Andy pays Bill $200.00 to release Bill's claims for damages incurred when Andy's truck damaged Bill's garage.

Releases can be very powerful documents. The various releases contained in this section are tailored to meet the most common situations in which a release is used. For a release to be valid, there must be some type of *consideration* (a promise to do or not do something) received by the person who is granting the release. The specific details of the particular consideration need not be specified in a release. Releases should be used carefully as they may prevent any future claims against the party to whom they are granted. In general, a release from claims relating to an accident that causes personal injury should not be signed without a prior examination by a doctor. Also note that a release relating to damage to community property in a "community property" state must be signed by both spouses. Study the various forms provided in back of this book to determine which one is proper for the use intended. Please note that the later section on *Promissory Notes* contains a Release of Promissory. *Note*: If you are at all unsure of the correct use of any forms in this section, please consult a competent attorney. The following releases are included in this section:

General Release: This release serves as a full blanket release of obligations from one party to another. It should only be used when all obligations of one party are to be released. The party signing this release is discharging the other party from all of their obligations to the signing party stemming from a specific incident or transaction. This form can be used when one party has a claim against a second party and the second agrees to waive the claim for payment.

Mutual Release: The mutual release form provides a method for two parties to jointly release each other from their mutual obligations or claims. This form should be used when both parties intend to discharge each other from all of their mutual obligations. It essentially serves the purpose of two mutual and reciprocal General Releases between two separate parties.

Specific Release: This release form should be used when only a particular claim or obligation is being released, while allowing other liabilities to continue. The obligation being released should be spelled out in careful and precise terms to prevent confusion with any other obligation or claim. In addition, the liabilities that are not being released but will survive, should also be carefully noted.

Receipts

In this section, various receipt forms are provided. In general, receipts are a formal acknowledgment of having received something, whether it is money or property. These forms do not have to be notarized. Please note that the later section on *Leases of Real Estate* contains a Receipt for Lease Security Deposit and a Rent Receipt to be used in conjunction with leases of real estate. The following receipt forms are included in this book:

Receipt in Full: This form should be used as a receipt for a payment that completely pays off a debt. You will need to include the amount paid, the name of the person who paid it, the date when paid, and a description of the obligation that is paid off (for example: an invoice, statement, or bill of sale). The original receipt should go to the person making the payment, but a copy should be retained.

Receipt on Account: This form should be used as a receipt for a payment that does not fully pay off a debt, but, rather, is a payment on account and is credited to the total balance due. You will need to include the amount paid, the name of the person who paid it, the date when paid, and a description of the account to which the payment is to be applied. The original receipt should go to the person making the payment, but a copy should be kept by you.

Receipt for Goods: This form should be used as a receipt for the acceptance of goods. It is intended to be used in conjunction with a delivery order or purchase order. It also states that the goods have been inspected and found to be in conformance with the order. The original of this receipt should be retained by the person delivering the goods and a copy should go to the person accepting delivery.

Note: If you are at all unsure of the correct use of any forms in this section, please consult a competent attorney.

Leases of Real Estate

A *lease* of real estate is simply a written contract for one party to rent a specific property from another for a certain amount and for a certain time period. As such, all of the general legal ramifications that relate to contracts also relate to leases. However, all states have additional requirements which pertain only to leases. If the rental period is to be for one year or more, most states require that leases be in writing. Leases can be prepared for *periodic* tenancies (that is, for example, month-to-month or week-to-week) or they can be for a *fixed* period (for example, from one specific date to another specific date). The residential lease contained in this book provides for a fixed-period tenancy. The Month-to-Month Rental Agreement in this book is a periodic tenancy.

There are also general guidelines for security deposits in most states. These most often follow a reasonable pattern and should be adhered to. Most states provide for the following with regard to lease security deposits:

- Security deposits should be no greater than one month's rent and should be fully refundable
- Security deposits should be used for the repair of damages only and not applied for the nonpayment of rent (an additional month's rent may be requested to cover potential nonpayment of rent situations)
- Security deposits should be kept in a separate, interest-bearing account and returned, with interest, to the tenant within 10 days of termination of a lease (minus, of course, any deductions for damages)

In addition to state laws regarding security deposits, many states have requirements relating to the time periods required prior to terminating a lease. These rules have evolved over time to prevent both the landlord or the tenant from being harmed by early termination of a lease. In general, if the lease is for a fixed time period, the termination of the lease is governed by the lease itself. Early termination of a fixed-period lease may, however, be governed by individual state law. For periodic leases (month-to-month, etc.), there are normally state rules as to how much advance notice must be given prior to the termination of a lease. Please check your state's listing in the Real Estate Law Appendix before using any of these forms. The forms in this section may be completed as tear-out forms or as text or PDF forms on the CD. *Note*: If you are at all unsure of the correct use of any forms in this section, please consult a competent attorney. The following forms are included in this section:

Residential Lease: This form should be used when renting a residential property. Note: Chicago and California residents must use additional forms that are provided on the CD. The following information will be necessary to prepare this form:

- The name and address of the landlord
- The name and address of the tenant
- A complete legal description of the leased property
- The length of time the lease will be in effect
- The amount of the rental payments
- The day of the month when the rent will be due
- The due date of the first rent payment
- The amount of the security deposit for damages
- The amount of additional rent held as rental default deposit
- Any utilities that the landlord will supply
- The utilities that the tenant will provide
- Any other additional terms; for example, no pets

Although the landlord and tenant can agree to any terms they desire, this particular lease provides for the following basic terms to be included:

- A fixed period term for the lease
- A security deposit for damages that will be returned within 10 days after the termination of the lease
- An additional month's rent as security for payment of the rent that will be returned within 10 days after the termination of the lease
- The tenant's agreement to keep the property in good repair and not make any alterations without consent
- The tenant's agreement not to assign the lease or sublet the property without the landlord's consent
- The landlord's right to inspect the property on a reasonable basis and that the tenant has already inspected it and found the property satisfactory
- The landlord's right to reenter and take possession on breach of the lease (in accordance with state law)
- That the landlord will provide tenant with the U.S. EPA lead pamphlet: "Protect Your Family from Lead in Your Home." *Note*: This document is only provided on the Forms-on-CD and is necessary *only* if the rental dwelling was built prior to 1978
- Any other additional terms that the parties agree upon

Month-to-Month Rental Agreement: This rental agreement provides for a month-to-month tenancy: one that continues each month indefinitely or until terminated by either party. For a fixed tenancy lease, please see the Residential Lease, explained above. Although the landlord and tenant can agree to any terms they desire, this particular lease provides for the following basic terms to be included:

- A month-to-month tenancy for the agreement
- A security deposit for damages, to be returned within 10 days after the termination of the agreement, but without interest unless required by state law
- An additional month's rent as security for payment of the rent, which will be returned within 10 days after the termination of the agreement, but without interest unless required by state law
- That the tenant agrees to keep the property in good repair and not make any alterations without consent
- Tenant agrees not to conduct any business without permission of the landlord
- Tenant agrees not to have any pets without permission of the landlord
- That landlord and tenant agree on who will pay utilities
- That the tenant agrees not to assign the agreement or sublet the property without the landlord's consent
- That the landlord has the right to inspect the property on a reasonable basis, and that the tenant has already inspected it and found it satisfactory

- That the landlord has the right to re-enter and take possession upon breach of the agreement (as long as it is in accordance with state law)
- That the landlord will provide tenant with the U.S. EPA lead pamphlet: "Protect Your Family from Lead in Your Home." *Note*: This document is only provided on the Forms-on-CD and is necessary *only* if the rental dwelling was built prior to 1978
- Any other additional terms that the parties agree upon

Amendment of Lease: Use this form to modify any terms of a lease (except for the expiration date, which is explained under "Extension of Lease" below). This amendment may be used to change any portion of the lease. Simply note what changes are being made in the appropriate place on this form. A copy of the original lease should be attached to this form. If a portion of the lease is being deleted, make note of the deletion. If certain language is being substituted, state the substitution clearly. If additional language is being added, make this clear. For example, you may wish to use language as follows:

- "Paragraph _____ is deleted from this lease"
- "Paragraph _____ is deleted from this lease and the following paragraph is substituted in its place:"
- "The following new paragraph is added to this lease:"

Extension of Lease: This document should be used to extend the effective time period during which a lease is in force. The use of this form allows the time limit to be extended without having to entirely redraft the lease. Under this document, all of the other terms of the lease will remain the same, with only the expiration date changing. You will need to fill in the original expiration date and the new expiration date. Other information necessary will be the names and addresses of the parties to the lease and a description of the lease. A copy of the original lease should be attached to this form.

Sublease: This form is used if the tenant subleases property covered by an original lease. This particular sublease form has both of the parties agreeing to indemnify and hold each other harmless for any failures to perform under the lease while they were the party liable under it. This indemnify and hold harmless clause simply means that if a claim arises for failure to perform, each party agrees to be responsible for the period of their own performance obligations. A description of the lease that is subleased should include the parties to the lease, a description of the property, and the date of the lease. Other information that is necessary to complete the sublease are the name and address of the original tenant, the name and address of the *subtenant* (the party to whom the property is being subleased), and the date of the sublease. A copy of the original lease should be attached to this form.

Consent to Sublease of Lease: This form is used if the original lease states that the consent of the landlord is necessary for a sublease to be valid. A description of the lease and the name and signature of the person giving the consent are all that is necessary for completing this form. A copy of the original lease should be attached to this form.

Notice of Breach of Lease: This form should be used to notify a party to a lease of the violation of a term of the lease or of an instance of failure to perform a required duty under the lease. It provides for a description of the alleged violation of the lease and for a time period in which the party is instructed to cure the breach of the lease. If the breach is not taken care of within the time period allowed, a lawyer should be consulted for further action, which may entail a lawsuit to enforce the lease terms. A copy of the original lease should be attached to this form.

Notice of Rent Default: This form allows for notice to a tenant of default in the payment of rent. It provides for the amount of the defaulted payments to be specified and for a time limit to be placed on payment before further action is taken. If the breach is not taken care of within the time period allowed, a lawyer should be consulted for further action, which may involve a lawsuit to enforce the lease terms. A copy of the original lease should be attached to this form.

Notice to Vacate Property: This notice informs a tenant who has already been notified of a breach of the lease (or of a late rent payment) to vacate the property. It sets a specific date by which the tenant must be out of the property. If the tenant fails to leave by the date set, an attorney should be consulted to begin eviction efforts.

Notice to Terminate Lease: By this notice, a landlord or tenant may inform the other of termination of a lease for breach of the lease. This action may be taken under the leases provided in this book because there are specific lease provisions that allow this action and (presumably) the landlord or tenant has agreed to these provisions. To complete this form, the lease should be described, the breach of the lease should be described, the date of the original Notice of Breach of Lease should be noted, and a date on which the tenant should deliver possession of the property to the landlord should be set.

Receipt for Lease Security Deposit: This form is to be used for receipt of a lease security deposit. The amount of the deposit and a description of the leased property are all that is necessary for completion.

Rent Receipt: This form may be used as a receipt for the periodic payment of rent. It provides for the amount paid, the period paid for, and a description of the property. Leases of personal property are often undertaken for the use of tools, equipment, or property necessary to perform a certain task. Other situations where such an agreement is often used is in the rental of property for recreational purposes. The needs of the parties for a personal property rental agreement depend a great deal on the type of property involved and the value of the property.

Rental of Personal Property

The basic form that is included in this book is a very simple rental agreement that can be used for short-term rentals of relatively inexpensive property. If you are at all unsure of the correct use of this form or you need a more complex Personal Property Rental Agreement, please consult a competent attorney.

Personal Property Rental Agreement: This form is designed to be used in situations involving inexpensive property for short terms. This form does not address many of the potential problems that may arise in the rental of personal property. However, this simple agreement does provide a legal basis for an enforceable contract between two parties regarding the rental of personal property. The information necessary for the preparation of this form are simply the names and addresses of the parties (the *owner* and the *renter*), a description of the property, and the amount and term of the rental.

Sale of Personal Property

The forms described in this section are for use when selling personal property. A contract for the sale of personal property may be part of a greater transaction (involving, for example, the sale of real estate or a complete business) or it may be prepared separate from any other dealings. A *bill of sale* provides a receipt for both parties that verifies that the sale has been completed and the delivery of the item in question has taken place. Bills of sale are often utilized to document the sale of personal property that is part of a real estate transaction when the terms of the sale are part of the real estate sales contract. *Note*: If you are at all unsure of the correct use of any forms in this section, please consult a competent attorney.

The following forms are provided in this section:

Contract for Sale of Personal Property: This form may be used for documenting the sale of any type of personal property. It may be used for vehicles, business assets, or any other personal property. The information necessary to complete this form are the names and addresses of the seller and the buyer, a complete description of the property being sold, the total purchase price, and the terms of the payment of this price.

Bill of Sale, with Warranties: This document is used as a receipt of the sale of personal property. It is, in many respects, often used to operate as a *title* (or ownership document) to items of personal property. It verifies that the person noted in the bill of sale has obtained legal title to the property from the previous owner. This particular version also provides that the seller *warrants* (or guarantees) that he or she has the authority to transfer legal title to the buyer and that there are no outstanding debts or liabilities for the property. In addition, this form provides that the seller warrants that the property is in good working condition on the date of the sale. To complete this form, simply fill in the names and addresses of the seller and buyer, the purchase price of the item, and a description of the property.

Bill of Sale, without Warranties: This form also provides a receipt to the buyer for the purchase of an item of personal property. However, in this form, the seller makes no warranties at all, either regarding the authority to sell the item or the condition of the item. It is sold to the buyer in "as is" condition. The buyer takes it regardless of any defects. To complete this form, fill in the names and addresses of the seller and buyer, the purchase price of the item, and a description of the property.

Bill of Sale, Subject to Debt: This form also provides a receipt to the buyer for the purchase of an item of personal property. This form, however, provides that the property sold is subject to a certain prior debt. It verifies that the seller has obtained legal title to the property from the previous owner, but that the seller specifies that the property is sold subject to a certain debt which the buyer is to pay off. In addition, the buyer agrees to indemnify the seller regarding any liability on the debt. This particular bill of sale version also provides that the seller warrants that he or she has authority to transfer legal title to the buyer. In addition, this form provides that the owner warrants that the property is in good working condition on the date of the sale. To complete this form, fill in the names and addresses of the seller and buyer, the purchase price of the item, a description of the property, and a description of the debt. You may wish to use this particular bill of sale in conjunction with a Promissory Note (discussed later).

Sale of Real Estate

In this section are various forms for the sale and transfer of real estate. Although most real estate sales today are handled by real estate professionals, it is still perfectly legal to buy and sell property without the use of a real estate broker or lawyer. The forms provided in this section allow an individual to prepare the necessary forms for many basic real estate transactions. Please note, however, that there may be various state and local variations on sales contracts, mortgages, or other real estate documents. Check the Apppendix on State Real Estate Laws on the CD first. If in doubt, please check with a local real estate professional or an attorney. *Note*: If you are at all unsure of the correct use of any forms in this section, please consult a competent attorney. The following forms are provided:

Agreement to Sell Real Estate: This form may be used for setting down an agreement to buy and sell property. It contains the basic clauses to cover situations that will arise in most typical real estate transactions. The following items are covered:

- The sale is contingent on the buyer being able to obtain financing 30 days prior to the closing
- If the sale is not completed, the buyer will be given back the earnest money deposit, without interest or penalty

- The seller will provide a Warranty Deed for the real estate and a Bill of Sale for any personal property included in the sale
- Certain items will be pro-rated and adjusted as of the closing date
- The buyer and the seller may split the various closing costs
- The seller discloses and the buyer acknowledges any known lead-based paint in the building
- The seller represents that he or she has good title to the property and that the personal property included is in good working order
- The title to the property will be verified by either title insurance or an abstract of title

In order to prepare this contract, the following information will be necessary:

- The names and addresses of the buyer and seller
- A description of the property involved
- The purchase price of the property
- How the purchase price will be paid
- The amount of earnest money paid on signing the contract
- The date, place, and time for closing the sale
- What documents will be required at closing
- Which items will be adjusted and pro-rated at closing
- Which closing costs will be paid for by the seller and which costs by the buyer
- Whether there are any outstanding claims, liabilities, or indebtedness pertaining to the property
- Seller's disclosure and buying acknowledgment of lead-based paint
- Whether there are any additional terms
- Which state's laws will be used to interpret the contract

Title insurance or an abstract of title will need to be obtained from a local title company or attorney. Finally, a Bill of Sale for any personal property (see above under *Sale of Personal Property*) and a Warranty Deed will need to be prepared for use at the closing of the sale. In addition, a lead warning brochure may be required. *Note*: This document is only provided on the Forms-on-CD and is necessary *only* if the residential dwelling was built prior to 1978

Option to Buy Real Estate Agreement: This form is designed to be used to offer an interested buyer a time period in which to have an exclusive option to purchase a parcel of real estate. It should be used in conjunction with a filled-in, but unsigned, copy of the above Agreement to Sell Real Estate. Through the use of this agreement, the seller can offer the buyer a time in which to consider the purchase without concern of a sale to another party. This agreement provides that in exchange for a payment (that will be applied to the purchase price if the option is exercised), the buyer is given a period of time to accept the terms of a completed real estate contract. If the buyer accepts the terms and exercises the option in writing, the seller agrees to complete the sale. If the option is not exercised, the seller is then free to sell the property on the market and retain the money paid for the option. To complete this form, you will need the following information:

- The names and addresses of the buyer and seller
- A description of the property involved
- The amount of money to be paid for the option
- The time limit of the option
- The purchase price of the property

In addition, an Agreement to Sell Real Estate covering the property subject to the option should be completed and attached to the option agreement. This attached contract will provide all of the essential terms of the actual agreement to sell the property. (Note: California residents must also use the Addendum to Real Estate Contract on the CD).

Quitclaim Deed: Any transfers of real estate must be in writing. This type of deed is intended to be used when the seller is merely selling whatever interest he or she may have in the property. By using a quitclaim deed, a seller is not, in any way, guaranteeing that he or she actually owns any interest in the property. This type of deed may be used to settle any claims that a person may have to a piece of real estate, to settle disputes over property, or to transfer property between co-owners. To prepare this deed, simply fill in the name and address of the person who prepared the deed and where the recorded deed should be sent, the names and addresses of the *grantor* (the one transferring the property) and the *grantee* (the one receiving the property) and the legal description of the property. For this deed form to be recorded, it must be properly notarized and witnessed.

Warranty Deed: This type of deed is used in most real estate situations. It provides that the seller is *conveying* (transferring) to the buyer a full and complete title to the land without any restrictions or debts (a *fee simple* title). If there are any restrictions or debts that the property will be subject to, these should be noted in the legal description area provided. To complete this deed, simply fill in the name and address of the person who prepared the deed and where the recorded deed should be sent, the names and addresses of the *grantor* (the one selling the property) and the *grantee* (the one buying the property) and the legal description of the property. For the transfer to actually take place, the grantor must give the actual deed to the grantee. In addition, in order for this document to be recorded, it should be properly notarized and witnessed.

Real Estate Disclosure Statements: This form is now required in many states for residential real estate sales. It provides for disclosures by the Seller to the Buyer of any known problems with the property in question. These forms are provided as state-specific forms only on the CD. Please check with your state's listing on the Appendix of State Real Estate Laws also included on the CD for information about your state's requirements.

Promissory Notes

Contained in this section are several types of promissory notes. A *promissory note* is a document by which a borrower promises to pay the holder of the note a certain amount of money under specific terms. In the forms in this section, the person who borrows the money is referred to as the *borrower* and the person whom the borrower is to pay is referred to as the *noteholder*. The noteholder is generally also the lender, but this need not be so. The forms in this section are intended for use only by individuals who are not regularly in the business of lending money. Complex state and federal regulations apply to lending institutions and such rules are beyond the scope of this book. This section also contains a form for the release of a promissory note. *Note*: If you are at all unsure of the correct use of any forms in this section, please consult a competent attorney.

Promissory Note (Installment Repayment): This type of promissory note is a standard unsecured note. Being *unsecured* means that the noteholder has no collateral or specific property to foreclose against should the borrower default on the note. If the borrower doesn't pay, the noteholder must sue and get a general judgment against the borrower. Collection of the judgment may then be made against the borrower's assets. This particular note calls for the borrower to pay a certain annual interest rate on the note and to make periodic payments to the noteholder. It also has certain general terms:

- The borrower may prepay any amount on the note without penalty
- If the borrower is in default, the noteholder may demand full payment on the note
- The note is not assumable by anyone other than the borrower
- The borrower waives certain formalities relating to demands for payment
- The borrower agrees to pay any of the costs of collection after a default

In order to complete this form, the following information is necessary:

- The names and addresses of the borrower and the noteholder
- The amount of the principal of the loan
- The annual interest rate to be charged
- The period for the installments (for example, monthly or weekly)
- The date of the period on which payments will be due
- The number of days a payment may be late before it is considered a default

Promissory Note (Lump Sum Repayment): This note is also an unsecured promise to pay. However, this version of a promissory note calls for the payment, including accrued interest, to be paid in one lump sum at a certain date in the future. This note has the same general conditions relating to prepayment, defaults, and assumability as the Promissory Note with Installment Payments discussed above. To prepare this form, use the following information:

- The names and addresses of the borrower and the noteholder
- The amount of the principal of the loan
- The annual interest rate to be charged
- The final due date of the lump sum payment
- The number of days past the due date that payment may be made before the note is in default

Promissory Note (on Demand): This also is an unsecured note. This type of promissory note, however, is immediately payable in full at any time upon the demand of the noteholder. This note has the same general conditions relating to prepayment, defaults, and assumability as the Promissory Note with Installment Payments discussed previously. The following information is necessary to complete this form:

- The names and addresses of the borrower and the noteholder
- The amount of the principal of the loan
- The annual interest rate to be charged
- The number of days past the demand date that payment may be made before the note is in default

Release of Promissory Note: This release is intended to be used to release a party from obligations under a Promissory Note. There are several other methods by which to accomplish this same objective. The return of the original note to the maker, clearly marked "Paid in Full" will serve the same purpose. A Receipt in Full will also accomplish this goal (see previous section on *Receipts*). The Release of Promissory Note may, however, be used in those situations when the release is based on something other than payment in full of the underlying note. For example, the note may be satisfied as a gift from the bearer of the note of release from the obligation. Another situation may involve a release of the note based on a concurrent release of a claim that the maker of the note holds against the holder of the note.

Contract

This Contract is made on _____ , 20 ____ ,
between _____ ,
address:

and _____ ,
address:

For valuable consideration, the parties agree as follows:

No modification of this Contract will be effective unless it is in writing and is signed by both parties. This Contract binds and benefits both parties and any successors. Time is of the essence of this contract. This document, including any attachments, is the entire agreement between the parties. This Contract is governed by the laws of the State of _____ .

The parties have signed this Contract on the date specified at the beginning of this Contract.

_____   _____
Signature   Signature

_____   _____
Printed Name   Printed Name

Extension of Contract

This Extension of Contract is made on _____ , 20 _____ ,
between _____ ,
address:

and _____ ,
address:

For valuable consideration, the parties agree as follows:

1. The following described contract will end on _____ , 20 _____ :

   This contract is attached to this Extension and is a part of this Extension.

2. The parties agree to extend this contract for an additional period, which will begin immediately on the expiration of the original time period and will end on _____ , 20 _____ .

3. The Extension of this contract will be on the same terms and conditions as the original contract. This Extension binds and benefits both parties and any successors. This document, including the attached original contract, is the entire agreement between the parties.

The parties have signed this Extension on the date specified at the beginning of this Extension of Contract.

_____   _____
Signature   Signature

_____   _____
Printed Name   Printed Name

Modification of Contract

This Modification of Contract is made on _____, 20 _____,
between _____,
address:

and _____,
address:

For valuable consideration, the parties agree as follows:

1. The following described contract is attached to this Modification and is made a part of this Modification:

2. The parties agree to modify this contract as follows:

3. All other terms and conditions of the original contract remain in effect without modification. This Modification binds and benefits both parties and any successors. This document, including the attached contract, is the entire agreement between the parties.

The parties have signed this Modification on the date specified at the beginning of this Modification of Contract.

_____   _____
Signature   Signature

_____   _____
Printed Name   Printed Name

Termination of Contract

This Termination of Contract is made on _____ , 20 ____ ,
between _____ ,
address:

and _____ ,
address:

For valuable consideration, the parties agree as follows:

1. The parties are currently bound under the terms of the following described contract, which is attached and is part of this Termination:

2. They agree to mutually terminate and cancel this contract effective on this date. This Termination Agreement will act as a mutual release of all obligations under this contract for both parties, as if the contract has not been entered into in the first place.

3. This Termination binds and benefits both partics and any successors. This document, including the attached contract being terminated, is the entire agreement between the parties.

The parties have signed this Termination on the date specified at the beginning of this Termination of Contract.

_____   _____
Signature   Signature

_____   _____
Printed Name   Printed Name

Contract Exhibit _____

This Contract Exhibit _____ is attached and made part of the following contract:

Contract Exhibit _____

This Contract Exhibit _____ is attached and made part of the following contract:

Limited Power of Attorney

Notice: This is an important document. Before signing this document, you should know these important facts. By signing this document, you are not giving up any powers or rights to control your finances and property yourself. In addition to your own powers and rights, you may be giving another person, your attorney-in-fact, broad powers to handle your finances and property. This limited power of attorney may give the person whom you designate (your "attorney-in-fact") broad powers to handle your finances and property, which may include powers to encumber, sell or otherwise dispose of any real or personal property without advance notice to you or approval by you. THE POWERS GRANTED WILL NOT EXIST AFTER YOU BECOME DISABLED, OR INCAPACITATED. This document does not authorize anyone to make medical or other health care decisions for you. If you own complex or special assets such as a business, or if there is anything about this form that you do not understand, you should ask a lawyer to explain this form to you before you sign it. If you wish to change your limited power of attorney, you must complete a new document and revoke this one. You may revoke this document at any time by destroying it, by directing another person to destroy it in your presence or by signing a written and dated statement expressing your intent to revoke this document. If you revoke this document, you should notify your attorney-in-fact and any other person to whom you have given a copy of the form. You also should notify all parties having custody of your assets. These parties have no responsibility to you unless you actually notify them of the revocation. If your attorney-in-fact is your spouse and your marriage is annulled, or you are divorced after signing this document, this document is invalid. Since some 3rd parties or some transactions may not permit use of this document, it is advisable to check in advance, if possible, for any special requirements that may be imposed. You should sign this form only if the attorney-in-fact that you appoint is reliable, trustworthy and competent to manage your affairs. This form must be signed by the Principal (the person appointing the attorney-in-fact), witnessed by two persons other than the notary public, and acknowledged by a notary public.

I, _____ (printed name), of (address)_____, as principal, do grant a limited and specific power of attorney to, and do hereby appoint _____ (printed name), of (address) _____ to act as my attorney-in-fact and to have the full power and authority to perform only the following acts on my behalf to the same extent that I could do so personally if I were personally present, with respect to the following matter to the extent that I am permitted by law to act through an agent: (list specific acts and/or restrictions)

If the attorney-in-fact named above is unable or unwilling to serve, I appoint _____ (printed name), of (address) _____ , to be my attorney-in-fact for all purposes hereunder.

To induce any third party to rely upon this power of attorney, I agree that any third party receiving a signed copy or facsimile of this power of attorney may rely upon such copy, and that revocation or termination of this power of attorney shall be ineffective as to such third party until actual notice or knowledge of such revocation or termination shall have been received by such third party. I, for myself and for my heirs, executors, legal representatives and assigns, agree to indemnify and hold harmless any such third party from any and all claims that may arise against such third party by reason of such third party having relied on the provisions of this power of attorney.

This power of attorney shall not be effective in the event of my future disability or incapacity. This limited grant of authority does not authorize my attorney-in-fact to make any decisions regarding my medical or health care. This power of attorney may be revoked by me at any time and is automatically revoked upon my death. My attorney-in-fact shall not be compensated for his or her services nor shall my attorney-in-fact be liable to me, my estate, heirs, successors, or assigns for acting or refraining from acting under this document, except for willful misconduct or gross negligence. My attorney-in-fact accepts this appointment and agrees to act in my best interest as he or she considers advisable. This grant of authority shall include the power and authority to perform any incidental acts which may be reasonably required in order to perform the specific acts stated above.

Dated: _____

Signature and Declaration of Principal

I, _____ (printed name), the principal, sign my name to this power of attorney this _____ day of _____ and, being first duly sworn, do declare to the undersigned authority that I sign and execute this instrument as my power of attorney and that I sign it willingly, or willingly direct another to sign for me, that I execute it as my free and voluntary act for the purposes expressed in the power of attorney and that I am eighteen years of age or older, of sound mind and under no constraint or undue influence.

_____
Signature of Principal

Witness Attestation

I, _____ (printed name), the first witness, and I, _____ (printed name), the second witness, sign my name to the foregoing power of attorney being first duly sworn and do declare to the undersigned authority that the principal signs and executes this instrument as his/her power of attorney and that he\she signs it willingly, or willingly directs another to sign for him/her, and that I, in the presence and hearing of the principal, sign this power of attorney as witness to the principal's signing and that to the best of my knowledge the principal is eighteen years of age or older, of sound mind and under no constraint or undue influence.

_____
Signature of First Witness

_____
Signature of Second Witness

Notary Acknowledgment

State of _____

County of _____

Subscribed, sworn to and acknowledged before me by _____, the Principal, and subscribed and sworn to before me by _____, and _____, the witnesses, this _____ _____ day of _____ .

_____
Notary Signature

Notary Public,
In and for the County of _____
State of _____
My commission expires: _____ Seal

Acknowledgment and Acceptance of Appointment as Attorney-in-Fact O

I, _____, (printed name) have read the attached power of attorney and am the person identified as the attorney-in-fact for the principal. I hereby acknowledge that I accept my appointment as attorney-in-fact and that when I act as agent I shall exercise the powers for the benefit of the principal; I shall keep the assets of the principal separate from my assets; I shall exercise reasonable caution and prudence; and I shall keep a full and accurate record of all actions, receipts and disbursements on behalf of the principal.

_____   _____
Signature of Attorney-in-Fact   Date

Acknowledgment and Acceptance of Appointment as Successor Attorney-in-Fact

I, _____, (printed name) have read the attached power of attorney and am the person identified as the successor attorney-in-fact for the principal. I hereby acknowledge that I accept my appointment as successor attorney-in-fact and that, in the absence of a specific provision to the contrary in the power of attorney, when I act as agent I shall exercise the powers for the benefit of the principal; I shall keep the assets of the principal separate from my assets; I shall exercise reasonable caution and prudence; and I shall keep a full and accurate record of all actions, receipts and disbursements on behalf of the principal.

_____   _____
Signature of Successor Attorney-in-Fact   Date

Durable Unlimited Power of Attorney
Effective Immediately

Notice to Adult Signing this Document: This is an important document. Before signing this document, you should know these important facts. By signing this document, you are not giving up any powers or rights to control your finances and property yourself. In addition to your own powers and rights, you are giving another person, your attorney-in-fact, broad powers to handle your finances and property, which may include powers to encumber, sell or otherwise dispose of any real or personal property without advance notice to you or approval by you. THE POWERS GRANTED UNDER THIS DOCUMENT ARE EFFECTIVE IMMEDIATELY AND WILL REMAIN IN EFFECT IF YOU BECOME DISABLED OR INCAPACITATED. This document does not authorize anyone to make medical or other health care decisions for you. If you own complex or special assets such as a business, or if there is anything about this form that you do not understand, you should ask a lawyer to explain this form to you before you sign it. If you wish to change your durable unlimited power of attorney, you must complete a new document and revoke this one. You have the right to revoke the designation of the attorney-in-fact and the right to revoke this entire document at any time and in any manner. You may revoke this document at any time by destroying it, by directing another person to destroy it in your presence or by signing a written and dated statement expressing your intent to revoke this document. If you revoke this document, you should notify your attorney-in-fact and any other person to whom you have given a copy of the form. You also should notify all parties having custody of your assets. These parties have no responsibility to you unless you actually notify them of the revocation. If your attorney-in-fact is your spouse and your marriage is annulled, or you are divorced after signing this document, this document may become invalid. Since some third parties or some transactions may not permit use of this document, it is advisable to check in advance, if possible, for any special requirements that may be imposed. You should sign this form only if the attorney-in- fact you name is reliable, trustworthy and competent to manage your affairs. Generally, you may designate any competent adult as the attorney-in-fact under this document.

I, _____ (printed name), of (address) _____, as principal, do appoint _____ (printed name), of (address) _____, as my attorney-in- fact to act in my name, place and stead in any way which I myself could do, if I were personally present, with respect to all of the following matters to the extent that I am permitted by law to act through an agent: I grant my attorney-in-fact the maximum power under law to perform any act on my behalf that I could do personally, including but not limited to, all acts relating to any and all of my financial transactions and/or business affairs including all banking and financial institution transactions, all real estate or personal property transactions, all insurance or annuity transactions, all claims and litigation, and any and all business transactions. **This power of attorney shall become effective immediately and shall remain in full effect upon my disability or incapacitation.** This power of attorney grants no power or authority regarding healthcare decisions to my designated attorney-in-fact.

If the attorney-in-fact named above is unable or unwilling to serve, then I appoint _____ (printed name), of ___ _____ (address), to be my successor attorney-in-fact for all purposes hereunder.

My attorney-in-fact is granted full and unlimited power to act on my behalf in the same manner as if I were personally present. My attorney-in-fact accepts this appointment and agrees to act in my best interest as he or she considers advisable. To induce any third party to rely upon this power of attorney, I agree that any third party receiving a signed copy or facsimile of this power of attorney may rely upon such copy, and that revocation or termination of this power of attorney shall be ineffective as to such third party until actual notice or knowledge of such revocation or termination shall have been received by such third party. I, for myself and for my heirs, executors, legal representatives and assigns, agree to indemnify and hold harmless any such third party from any and all claims that may arise against such third party by reason of such third party having relied on the provisions of this power of attorney. This power of attorney may be revoked by me at any time and is automatically revoked upon my death.

My attorney-in-fact shall not be compensated for his or her services nor shall my attorney-in-fact be liable to me, my estate, heirs, successors, or assigns for acting or refraining from acting under this document, except for willful misconduct or gross negligence. Revocation of this document is not effective unless a third party has actual knowledge of such revocation.

I intend for my attorney-in-fact under this Power of Attorney to be treated as I would be with respect to my rights regarding the use and disclosure of my individually identifiable health information or other medical records. This release authority applies to any information governed by the Health Insurance Portability and Accountability Act of 1996 (aka HIPAA), 42 USC 1320d and 45 CFR 160-164.

Signature and Declaration of Principal

I, _____(printed name), the principal, sign my name to this power of attorney this _____ day of _____and, being first duly sworn, do declare to the undersigned authority that I sign and execute this instrument as my power of attorney and that I sign it willingly, or willingly direct another to sign for me, that I execute it as my free and voluntary act for the purposes expressed in the power of attorney and that I am eighteen years of age or older, of sound mind and under no constraint or undue influence ,and that I have read and understand the contents of the notice at the beginning of this document.

_____
Signature of Principal

Witness Attestation

I, _____ (printed name), the first witness, and
I, _____ (printed name), the second witness,
sign my name to the foregoing power of attorney being first duly sworn and do declare to the undersigned authority that the principal signs and executes this instrument as his/her power of attorney and that he/she signs it willingly, or willingly directs another to sign for him/her, and that I, in the presence and hearing of the principal, sign this power of attorney as witness to the principal's signing and that to the best of my knowledge the principal is eighteen years of age or older, of sound mind and under no constraint or undue influence.

_____
Signature of First Witness

_____
Signature of Second Witness

Notary Acknowledgment

The State of _____
County of _____
Subscribed, sworn to and acknowledged before me by _____,
the principal, and subscribed and sworn to before me by _____, the
first witness, and _____, the second witness on this date _____
_____.

_____
Notary Public Signature
Notary Public, In and for the County of _____ State of _____
My commission expires: _____ Notary Seal

Acknowledgment and Acceptance of Appointment as Attorney-in-Fact

I, _____, (printed name) have read the attached power of attorney and am the person identified as the attorney-in-fact for the principal. I hereby acknowledge that I accept my appointment as attorney-in-fact and that when I act as agent I shall exercise the powers for the benefit of the principal; I shall keep the assets of the principal separate from my assets; I shall exercise reasonable caution and prudence; and I shall keep a full and accurate record of all actions, receipts and disbursements on behalf of the principal.

_____   _____
Signature of Attorney-in-Fact   Date

Acknowledgment and Acceptance of Appointment as Successor Attorney-in-Fact

I, _____, (printed name) have read the attached power of attorney and am the person identified as the successor attorney-in-fact for the principal. I hereby acknowledge that I accept my appointment as successor attorney-in-fact and that, in the absence of a specific provision to the contrary in the power of attorney, when I act as agent I shall exercise the powers for the benefit of the principal; I shall keep the assets of the principal separate from my assets; I shall exercise reasonable caution and prudence; and I shall keep a full and accurate record of all actions, receipts and disbursements on behalf of the principal.

_____　　　_____
Signature of Successor Attorney-in-Fact　　　　　　　　Date

Durable Unlimited Power of Attorney
Effective upon Disability

Notice to Adult Signing this Document: This is an important document. Before signing this document, you should know these important facts. By signing this document, you are not giving up any powers or rights to control your finances and property yourself. In addition to your own powers and rights, you are giving another person, your attorney-in-fact, broad powers to handle your finances and property, which may include powers to encumber, sell or otherwise dispose of any real or personal property without advance notice to you or approval by you. THE POWERS GRANTED UNDER THIS DOCUMENT WILL ONLY GO INTO EFFECT IF YOU BECOME DISABLED OR INCAPACITATED, AS CERTIFIED BY YOUR PRIMARY PHYSICIAN, OR BY ANOTHER ATTENDING PHYSICIAN, IF YOUR PRIMARY PHYSICIAN IS NOT AVAILABLE. This document does not authorize anyone to make medical or other health care decisions for you. If you own complex or special assets such as a business, or if there is anything about this form that you do not understand, you should ask a lawyer to explain this form to you before you sign it. If you wish to change your durable unlimited power of attorney, you must complete a new document and revoke this one. You have the right to revoke the designation of the attorney-in-fact and the right to revoke this entire document at any time and in any manner. You may revoke this document at any time by destroying it, by directing another person to destroy it in your presence or by signing a written and dated statement expressing your intent to revoke this document. If you revoke this document, you should notify your attorney-in-fact and any other person to whom you have given a copy of the form. You also should notify all parties having custody of your assets. These parties have no responsibility to you unless you actually notify them of the revocation. If your attorney-in-fact is your spouse and your marriage is annulled, or you are divorced after signing this document, this document may become invalid. Since some third parties or some transactions may not permit use of this document, it is advisable to check in advance, if possible, for any special requirements that may be imposed. You should sign this form only if the attorney-in-fact you name is reliable, trustworthy and competent to manage your affairs. Generally, you may designate any competent adult as the attorney-in-fact under this document.

I, _____(printed name), of (address) _____, as principal, do appoint _____(printed name), of (address) _____, as my attorney-in-fact to act in my name, place and stead in any way which I myself could do, if I were personally present, with respect to all of the following matters to the extent that I am permitted by law to act through an agent: I grant my attorney-in-fact the maximum power under law to perform any act on my behalf that I could do personally, including but not limited to, all acts relating to any and all of my financial transactions and/or business affairs including all banking and financial institution transactions, all real estate or personal property transactions, all insurance or annuity transactions, all claims and litigation, and any and all business transactions. This power of attorney shall only become effective upon my disability or incapacitation, as certified by my primary physician, or if my primary physician is not available, by any other attending physician. This power of attorney grants no power or authority regarding healthcare decisions to my designated attorney-in-fact.

If the attorney-in-fact named above is unable or unwilling to serve, then I appoint _____(printed name), of _____ (address), to be my successor attorney-in-fact for all purposes hereunder.

My attorney-in-fact is granted full and unlimited power to act on my behalf in the same manner as if I were personally present. My attorney-in-fact accepts this appointment and agrees to act in my best interest as he or she considers advisable. To induce any third party to rely upon this power of attorney, I agree that any third party receiving a signed copy or facsimile of this power of attorney may rely upon such copy, and that revocation or termination of this power of attorney shall be ineffective as to such third party until actual notice or knowledge of such revocation or termination shall have been received by such third party. I, for myself and for my heirs, executors, legal representatives and assigns, agree to indemnify and hold harmless any such third party from any and all claims that may arise against such third party by reason of such third party having relied on the provisions of this power of attorney. This power of attorney may be revoked by me at any time and is automatically revoked upon my death. My attorney-in-fact shall not be compensated for his or her services nor shall my attorney-in-fact be liable to me, my estate, heirs, successors, or assigns for acting or refraining from acting under this document, except for willful misconduct or gross negligence. Revocation of this document is not effective unless a third party has actual knowledge of such revocation.

I intend for my attorney-in-fact under this Power of Attorney to be treated as I would be with respect to my rights regarding the use and disclosure of my individually identifiable health information or other medical records. This release authority applies to any information governed by the Health Insurance Portability and Accountability Act of 1996 (aka HIPAA), 42 USC 1320d and 45 CFR 160-164.

Signature and Declaration of Principal

I, _____ (printed name), the principal, sign my name to this power of attorney this _____day of _____and, being first duly sworn, do declare to the undersigned authority that I sign and execute this instrument as my power of attorney and that I sign it willingly, or willingly direct another to sign for me, that I execute it as my free and voluntary act for the purposes expressed in the power of attorney and that I am eighteen years of age or older, of sound mind and under no constraint or undue influence ,and that I have read and understand the contents of the notice at the beginning of this document.

_____
Signature of Principal

Witness Attestation

I, _____ (printed name), the first witness, and
I, _____ (printed name), the second witness, sign my name to the foregoing power of attorney being first duly sworn and do declare to the undersigned authority that the principal signs and executes this instrument as his/her power of attorney and that he/she signs it willingly, or willingly directs another to sign for him/her, and that I, in the presence and hearing of the principal, sign this power of attorney as witness to the principal's signing and that to the best of my knowledge the principal is eighteen years of age or older, of sound mind and under no constraint or undue influence.

_____   _____
Signature of First Witness   Signature of Second Witness

Notary Acknowledgment

The State of _____
County of _____
Subscribed, sworn to and acknowledged before me by _____, the principal, and subscribed and sworn to before me by _____, the first witness, and _____, the second witness on this date _____.

_____
Notary Public Signature
Notary Public, In and for the County of _____   State of _____
My commission expires: _____   Notary Seal

Acknowledgment and Acceptance of Appointment as Attorney-in-Fact

I, _____ (printed name) have read the attached power of attorney and am the person identified as the attorney-in-fact for the principal. I hereby acknowledge that I accept my appointment as attorney-in-fact and that when I act as agent I shall exercise the powers for the benefit of the principal; I shall keep the assets of the principal separate from my assets; I shall exercise reasonable caution and prudence; and I shall keep a full and accurate record of all actions, receipts and disbursements on behalf of the principal.

_____   _____
Signature of Attorney-in-Fact   Date

Acknowledgment and Acceptance of Appointment as Successor Attorney-in-Fact

I, _____ (printed name) have read the attached power of attorney and am the person identified as the successor attorney-in-fact for the principal. I hereby acknowledge that I accept my appointment as successor attorney-in-fact and that, in the absence of a specific provision to the contrary in the power of attorney, when I act as agent I shall exercise the powers for the benefit of the principal; I shall keep the assets of the principal separate from my assets; I shall exercise reasonable caution and prudence; and I shall keep a full and accurate record of all actions, receipts and disbursements on behalf of the principal.

_____   _____
Signature of Successor Attorney-in-Fact   Date

Durable Health Care Power of Attorney and Appointment of Health Care Agent and Proxy

NOTICE TO ADULT SIGNING THIS DOCUMENT: This is an important legal document. Before executing this document, you should know these facts: This document gives the person you designate (the attorney-in-fact) the power to make MOST health care decisions for you if you lose the capacity to make informed health care decisions for yourself. This power is effective only when your attending physician determines that you have lost the capacity to make informed health care decisions for yourself. Regardless of this document, as long as you have the capacity to make informed health care decisions for yourself, you retain the right to make all medical and other health care decisions for yourself. You may include specific limitations in this document on the authority of the attorney-in-fact to make health care decisions for you. Subject to any specific limitations you include in this document, if your attending physician determines that you have lost the capacity to make an informed decision on a health care matter, the attorney-in-fact GENERALLY will be authorized by this document to make health care decisions for you to the same extent as you could make those decisions yourself, if you had the capacity to do so. The authority of the attorney-in-fact to make health care decisions for you GENERALLY will include the authority to give informed consent, to refuse to give informed consent, or to withdraw informed consent to any care, treatment, service, or procedure to maintain, diagnose, or treat a physical or mental condition. Additionally, when exercising authority to make health care decisions for you, the attorney-in-fact will have to act consistently with your desires or, if your desires are unknown, to act in your best interest. You may express your desires to the attorney-in-fact by including them in this document or by making them known to the attorney-in-fact in another manner. When acting pursuant to this document, the attorney-in-fact GENERALLY will have the same rights that you have to receive information about proposed health care, to review health care records, and to consent to the disclosure of health care records. You can limit that right in this document if you so choose. GENERALLY, you may designate any competent adult as the attorney-in-fact under this document. You have the right to revoke the designation of the attorney-in-fact and the right to revoke this entire document at any time and in any manner. Any such revocation generally will be effective when you express your intention to make the revocation. However, if you made your attending physician aware of this document, any such revocation will be effective only when you communicate it to your attending physician, or when a witness to the revocation or other health care personnel to whom the revocation is communicated by such a witness communicates it to your attending physician. If you execute this document and create a valid Health Care Power of Attorney with it, this will revoke any prior, valid power of attorney for health care that you created, unless you indicate otherwise in this document. This document is not valid as a Health Care Power of Attorney unless it is acknowledged before a notary public or is signed by at least two adult witnesses who are present when you sign or acknowledge your signature. No person who is related to you by blood, marriage, or adoption may be a witness. The attorney-in-fact, your attending physician, and the administrator of any nursing home in which you are receiving care also are ineligible to be witnesses. If there is anything in this document that you do not understand, you should ask a lawyer to explain it to you.

I, _____ (printed name), residing at _____, appoint the following person as my attorney-in-fact for health care decisions, my health care agent, and confer upon this person my health care proxy. This person shall hereafter referred to as my "health care representative":
_____ (printed name), residing at _____.

I grant my health care representative the maximum power under law to perform any acts on my behalf regarding health care matters that I could do personally under the laws of the State of _____ _____, including specifically the power to make any health decisions on my behalf, upon the terms and conditions set forth below. My health care representative accepts this appointment and agrees to act in my best interest as he or she considers advisable. This health care power of attorney and appointment of health care agent and proxy may be revoked by me at any time and is automatically revoked on my death. However, this power of attorney shall not be affected by my present or future disability or incapacity.

This health care power of attorney and appointment of health care agent and proxy has the following terms and conditions:

If I have signed a Living Will or Directive to Physicians, and it is still in effect, I direct that my health care representative abide by the directions that I have set out in that document. If at any time I should have an incurable injury, disease, or illness which has been certified as a terminal condition by my attending physician and one additional physician, both of whom have personally examined me, and such physicians have determined that there can be no recovery from such condition and my death is imminent, and where the application of life prolonging procedures would serve only to artificially prolong the dying process, then:

I direct my health care representative to assure that such procedures be withheld or withdrawn, and that I be permitted to die naturally with only the administration of medication, the administration of nutrition and/or hydration, or the performance of any medical procedure deemed necessary to provide me with comfort, care, or to alleviate pain. If at any time I should have been diagnosed as being in a persistent vegetative state which has been certified as incurable by my attending physician and one additional physician, both of whom have personally examined me, and such physicians have determined that there can be no recovery from such condition, and where the application of life prolonging procedures would serve only to artificially prolong the dying process, then: I direct that my health care representative assure that such procedures be withheld or withdrawn, and that I be permitted to die naturally with only the administration of medication, the administration of nutrition and/or hydration, or the performance of any medical procedure deemed necessary to provide me with comfort, care, or to alleviate pain.

THE FOLLOWING INSTRUCTIONS (IN BOLDFACE TYPE) ONLY APPLY IF I HAVE SIGNED MY NAME IN THIS SPACE: _____

However, if at any time I should have been diagnosed as being in a persistent vegetative state which has been certified as incurable by my attending physician and one additional physician, both of whom have personally examined me, and such physicians

have determined that there can be no recovery from such condition, I also direct that my health care representative have sole authority to order the withholding of any aid, including the administration of nutrition, hydration, and any other medical procedure deemed necessary to provide me with comfort, care, or to alleviate pain.

If I am able to communicate in any manner, including even blinking my eyes, I direct that my health care representative try and discuss with me the specifics of any proposed health care decision.

If I have any further terms or conditions, I state them here:

I have discussed my health care wishes with the person whom I have herein appointed as my health care representative, I am fully satisfied that the person who I have herein appointed as my health care representative will know my wishes with respect to my health care and I have full faith and confidence in their good judgement.

I further direct that my health care representative shall have full authority to do the following, should I lack the capacity to make such a decision myself, provided however, that this listing shall in no way limit the full authority that I give my health care representative to make health care decisions on my behalf:
    a. to give informed consent to any health care procedure;
    b. to sign any documents necessary to carry out or withhold any health care procedures on my behalf, including any waivers or releases of liabilities required by any health care provider;
    c. to give or withhold consent for any health care or treatment;
    d. to revoke or change any consent previously given or implied by law for any health care treatment;
    e. to arrange for or authorize my placement or removal from any health care facility or institution;
    f. to require that any procedures be discontinued, including the withholding of any medical treatment and/or aid, including the administration of nutrition, hydration, and any other medical procedure deemed necessary to provide me with comfort, care, or to alleviate pain, subject to the conditions earlier provided in this document;
    g. to authorize the administration of pain-relieving drugs, even if they may shorten my life.

I desire that my wishes with respect to all health care matters be carried out through the authority that I have herein provided to my health care representative, despite any contrary wishes, beliefs, or opinions of any members of my family, relatives, or friends. I have read the Notice that precedes this document. I understand the full importance of this appointment, and I am emotionally and mentally competent to make this appointment of health care representative. I intend for my health care representative to be treated as I would be with respect to my rights regarding the use and disclosure of my individually identifiable health information or other medical records. This release authority applies to any information governed by the Health Insurance Portability and Accountability Act of 1996 (aka HIPAA), 42 USC 1320d and 45 CFR 160-164.

I declare to the undersigned authority that I sign and execute this instrument as my health care power of attorney and that I sign it willingly, or willingly direct another to sign for me, that I execute it as my free and voluntary act for the purposes expressed in this document and that I am nineteen years of age or older, of sound mind and under no constraint or undue influence ,and that I have read and understand the contents of the notice at the beginning of this document, and .that I understand the purpose and effect of this document.

Dated _____ , 20_____

_____
Signature of person granting health care power of attorney and appointing health care representative

_____
Printed name of person granting health care power of attorney and appointing health care representative

Witness Attestation

I, _____(printed name), the first witness, and
I, _____(printed name), the second witness, sign my name to the foregoing power of attorney being first duly sworn and do declare to the undersigned authority that the principal signs and executes this instrument as his/her power of attorney and that he/she signs it willingly, or willingly directs another to sign for him/her, and that I, in the presence and hearing of the principal, sign this power of attorney as witness to the principal's signing and that to the best of my knowledge the principal is nineteen years of age or older, of sound mind and under no constraint or undue influence. I am nineteen years of age or older. I am not appointed as the health care representative or attorney-in-fact by this document. I am not related to the principal by blood, adoption or marriage, nor am I entitled to any portion of the principal's estate under the laws of intestate succession or under any will or codicil of the principal. I also do not provide health care services to the principal, nor an employee of any health care facility in which the principal is a patient and am not financially responsible for the principal's health care.

_____   _____
Signature of First Witness   Address of First Witness

_____   _____
Signature of Second Witness   Address of Second Witness

Notary Acknowledgment

State of _____   County of _____

Subscribed, sworn to and acknowledged before me on this date _____ , 20_____ by _____ , the principal, who came before me personally, and under oath, stated that he or she is the person described in the above document and he or she signed the above document in my presence, or willingly directed another to sign for him or her. I declare under penalty of perjury that the person whose name is subscribed to this instrument appears to be of sound mind and under no duress, fraud, or undue influence. This document was also subscribed and sworn to before me on this date by _____, the first witness, and _____,the second witness .

_____
Notary Signature
Notary Public
In and for the County of _____   State of _____
My commission expires: _____   Notary Seal

In California, Delaware, Georgia, and Vermont, the following statement is required to be signed by a patient advocate, ombudsman (in California, Delaware and Vermont) or facility director (in Georgia or Vermont, if the principal is a patient in a skilled nursing facility:

Statement of Patient Advocate or Ombudsman

I declare under penalty of perjury under the laws of the State of _____
that I am a patient advocate or ombudsman (or medical facility director) and am serving as a witness required by the laws of this state and that the principal appeared to be of sound mind and under no duress, fraud, or undue influence.
Dated _____

_____   _____
Signature of Patient Advocate or Ombudsman   Printed name and title of witness

Acceptance of Appointment as Health Care Attorney-in-Fact and
Health Care Representative

I have read the attached durable health care power of attorney and am the person identified as the attorney-in-fact and health care representative for the principal. I hereby acknowledge that I accept my appointment as health care attorney-in-fact and health care representative and that when I act as agent I shall exercise the powers in the best interests of the principal.

_____
Signature of person granted health care power of attorney and appointed as health care representative

_____
Printed name of person granted health care power of attorney and appointed as health care representative

Revocation of Power of Attorney

I, _____,
address:

revoke the power of attorney dated _____,
which was granted to _____,
address:

to act as my attorney-in-fact.

Dated _____, 20 _____

_____
Signature of Person Revoking Power of Attorney

_____
Printed Name of Person Revoking Power of Attorney

Notary Acknowledgment

State of _____
County of _____

On _____, 20 _____, _____ personally came before me and, being duly sworn, did state that he or she is the person described in the above document and that he or she signed the above document in my presence.

_____
Signature of Notary Public

Notary Public, In and for the County of _____
State of _____

My commission expires: _____   Notary Seal

Will for Person with Children (Using Children's Trust)

Last Will and Testament of _____

I, _____, whose address is
_____,
declare that this is my Last Will and Testament and I revoke all previous wills.

My marital status is that:

I have _____ child(ren) living. His/Her/Their name(s), address(es), and date(s) of birth is/are as follows:

I have _____ grandchild(ren) living. His/Her/Their name(s), address(es), and date(s) of birth is/are as follows:

I make the following specific gifts:

I give _____,
to _____,
my _____,
or if not surviving, then to _____,
my _____.

I give _____,
to _____,
my _____,
or if not surviving, then to _____,
my _____.

I give _____,
to _____,
my _____,
or if not surviving, then to _____,
my _____.

I give _____,
to _____,
my _____,
or if not surviving, then to _____,
my _____.

I give _____,
to _____,
my _____,
or if not surviving, then to _____,
my _____.

I give _____,
to _____,
my _____,
or if not surviving, then to _____,
my _____.

I give _____,
to _____,
my _____,
or if not surviving, then to _____,
my _____.

I give all the rest of my property, whether real or personal, wherever located,
to _____,
my _____,
or if not surviving, to _____,
my _____.

All beneficiaries named in this will must survive me by thirty (30) days to receive any gift under this will. If any beneficiary and I should die simultaneously, I shall be conclusively presumed to have survived that beneficiary for purposes of this will.

I appoint _____,
my _____,
of _____,
as Executor, to serve without bond. If not surviving or otherwise unable to serve,
I appoint _____,
my _____,
of _____,
as Alternate Executor, also to serve without bond. In addition to any powers, authority, and discretion granted by law, I grant such Executor or Alternate Executor any and all powers to perform any acts, in his/her sole discretion and without court approval, for the management and distribution of my estate, including independent administration of my estate.

If a Guardian is needed for my/any of my minor child(ren),
I appoint _____,
my _____,
of _____,
as Guardian of the person(s) and property of my/any of my minor child(ren), to serve without bond. If not surviving, or unable to serve,
I appoint _____,
my _____,
of _____,
as Alternate Guardian, also to serve without bond. In addition to any powers, authority, and discretion granted by law, I grant such Guardian or Alternate Guardian any and all powers to perform any acts, in his/her sole discretion and without court approval, for the management and distribution of the property of my/any of my minor child(ren).

If my/any of my child(ren) is/are under _____ years of age, upon my death, I direct that any property that I give him/her/them under this will be held in an individual trust for my/each child(ren), under the following terms, until he/she/each shall reach _____ years of age.

In addition, I appoint _____,
my _____,
of _____,
as Trustee of any and all required trusts, to serve without bond. If not surviving, or otherwise unable to serve, then I appoint _____,
my _____,
of _____,
as Alternate Trustee, also to serve without bond. In addition to all powers, authority, and discretion granted by law, I grant such Trustee or Alternate Trustee full power to perform any act, in his/her sole discretion and without court approval, to distribute and manage the assets of any such trust.

In the Trustee's sole discretion, the Trustee may distribute any or all of the principal, income, or both, of any such trust as deemed necessary for the beneficiary's health, support, welfare, and education. Any income not distributed shall be added to the trust principal.

Any such trust shall terminate when the beneficiary reaches the required age, when the beneficiary dies prior to reaching the required age, or when all trust funds have been distributed. Upon termination, any remaining undistributed principal and income shall pass to the beneficiary; or if not surviving, to the beneficiary's heirs; or if none, to the residue of my estate.

I also declare that, pursuant to the Uniform Anatomical Gift Act, I donate any of my body parts and/or organs to any medical institution willing to accept and use them, and I direct my Executor to carry out such donation.

Funeral arrangements have been made with the _____,
of _____,
for burial at _____,
located in _____,

and I direct my Executor to carry out such arrangements.

I publish and sign this Last Will and Testament, consisting of ____ typewritten pages, on _____ , 20 _____ , and declare that I do so freely, for the purposes expressed, under no constraint or undue influence, and that I am of sound mind and of legal age.

_____   _____
Signature of Testator   Printed Name of Testator

We, the undersigned, being first sworn on oath and under penalty of perjury, state that:

On _____ , 20 _____ , in the presence of all of us, the above-named Testator published and signed this Last Will and Testament, and then at Testator's request, and in Testator's presence, and in each other's presence, we all signed below as witnesses, and we declare, under penalty of perjury, that, to the best of our knowledge, the Testator signed this instrument freely, under no constraint or undue influence, and is of sound mind and legal age.

_____
Signature of Witness #1

_____
Printed Name of Witness #1

_____
Address of Witness #1

_____
Signature of Witness #3

_____
Printed Name of Witness #3

_____
Address of Witness #3

_____
Signature of Witness #2

_____
Printed Name of Witness #2

_____
Address of Witness #2

Notary Acknowledgment

State of _____
County of _____

On _____ , 20 _____ , _____ , the Testator, and _____ , _____ , and _____ , the witnesses, personally came before me and, being duly sworn, did state that they are the persons described in the above document and that they signed the above document in my presence as a free and voluntary act for the purposes stated.

_____
Signature of Notary Public

Notary Public, In and for the County of _____
State of _____

My commission expires: _____   Notary Seal

Page ___ of ___ pages   Testator's initials _____

Will for Person with No Children

Last Will and Testament of _____

I, _____, whose address is
_____,
declare that this is my Last Will and Testament and I revoke all previous wills.

My marital status is that:

I have no children or grandchildren living.

I make the following specific gifts:

I give _____,
to _____,
my _____,
or if not surviving, then to _____,
my _____.

I give _____,
to _____,
my _____,
or if not surviving, then to _____,
my _____.

I give _____,
to _____,
my _____,
or if not surviving, then to _____,
my _____.

I give _____,
to _____,
my _____,
or if not surviving, then to _____,
my _____.

I give all the rest of my property, whether real or personal, wherever located,
to _____,
my _____,
or if not surviving, to _____,
 my _____.

All beneficiaries named in this will must survive me by thirty (30) days to receive any gift under this will. If any beneficiary and I should die simultaneously, I shall be conclusively presumed to have survived that beneficiary for purposes of this will.

I appoint _____,
my _____,
of _____,
as Executor, to serve without bond. If not surviving or otherwise unable to serve,
I appoint _____,
my _____,
of _____,
as Alternate Executor, also to serve without bond. In addition to any powers, authority, and discretion granted by law, I grant such Executor or Alternate Executor any and all powers to perform any acts, in his/her sole discretion and without court approval, for the management and distribution of my estate, including independent administration of my estate.

I also declare that, pursuant to the Uniform Anatomical Gift Act, I donate any of my body parts and/or organs to any medical institution willing to accept and use them, and I direct my Executor to carry out such donation.

Funeral arrangements have been made with the_____,
of _____,
for burial at _____,
located in _____,

and I direct my Executor to carry out such arrangements.

I publish and sign this Last Will and Testament, consisting of ____ typewritten pages, on _____ , 20 _____ , and declare that I do so freely, for the purposes expressed, under no constraint or undue influence, and that I am of sound mind and of legal age.

_____   _____
Signature of Testator   Printed Name of Testator

Page ___ of ___ pages   Testator's initials _____

We, the undersigned, being first sworn on oath and under penalty of perjury, state that:

On _____ , 20 _____ , in the presence of all of us, the above-named Testator published and signed this Last Will and Testament, and then at Testator's request, and in Testator's presence, and in each other's presence, we all signed below as witnesses, and we declare, under penalty of perjury, that, to the best of our knowledge, the Testator signed this instrument freely, under no constraint or undue influence, and is of sound mind and legal age.

_____ _____
Signature of Witness #1   Signature of Witness #3

_____ _____
Printed Name of Witness #1   Printed Name of Witness #3

_____ _____
Address of Witness #1   Address of Witness #3

_____
Signature of Witness #2

_____
Printed Name of Witness #2

_____
Address of Witness #2

Notary Acknowledgment

State of _____
County of _____

On _____ , 20 _____ , _____ , the Testator, and _____ , _____ , and _____ , the witnesses, personally came before me and, being duly sworn, did state that they are the persons described in the above document and that they signed the above document in my presence as a free and voluntary act for the purposes stated.

_____
Signature of Notary Public

Notary Public, In and for the County of _____
State of _____

My commission expires: _____   Notary Seal

Page ___ of ___ pages   Testator's initials _____

Living Will Declaration and Directive to Physicians of _____

Notice to Adult Signing This Document: This is an important legal document. This document directs the medical treatment you are to receive in the event you are unable to participate in your own medical decisions and you are in a terminal condition. This document may state what kind of treatment you want or do not want to receive. This document can control whether you live or die. Prepare this document carefully. If you use this form, read it completely. You may want to seek professional help to make sure the form does what you intend and is completed without mistakes. This document will remain valid and in effect until and unless you revoke it. Review this document periodically to make sure it continues to reflect your wishes. You may amend or revoke this document at any time by notifying your physician and other health-care providers. You should give copies of this document to your physician and your family. This form is entirely optional. If you choose to use this form, please note that the form provides signature lines for you, the three witnesses whom you have selected and a notary public.

I, _____ , being of sound mind, willfully and voluntarily make known my desire that my life not be artificially prolonged under the circumstances set forth below, and, pursuant to any and all applicable laws in the State of _____ , I declare that:

If at any time I should have an incurable injury, disease, or illness which has been certified as a terminal condition by my attending physician and one additional physician, both of whom have personally examined me, and such physicians have determined that there can be no recovery from such condition and my death is imminent, and where the application of life prolonging procedures would serve only to artificially prolong the dying process, then:

I direct that such procedures be withheld or withdrawn, and that I be permitted to die naturally with only the administration of medication, the administration of nutrition and/or hydration, or the performance of any medical procedure deemed necessary to provide me with comfort, care, or to alleviate pain.

If at any time I should have been diagnosed as being in a persistent vegetative state which has been certified as incurable by my attending physician and one additional physician, both of whom have personally examined me, and such physicians have determined that there can be no recovery from such condition, and where the application of life prolonging procedures would serve only to artificially prolong the dying process, then:

I direct that such procedures be withheld or withdrawn, and that I be permitted to die naturally with only the administration of medication, the administration of nutrition and/or hydration, or the performance of any medical procedure deemed necessary to provide me with comfort, care, or to alleviate pain.

In the absence of my ability to give directions regarding my treatment in the above situations, including directions regarding the use of such life prolonging procedures, then:

It is my intention that this declaration shall be honored by my family, my physician, and any court of law, as the final expression of my legal right to refuse medical and surgical treatment. I declare that I fully accept the consequences for such refusal.

If I have any additional directions, I will state them here:

If I have also signed a Health Care Power of Attorney, Appointment of Health Care Agent, or Health Care Proxy, I direct the person who I have appointed with such instrument to follow the directions that I have made in this document. I intend for my agent to be treated as I would be with respect to my rights regarding the use and disclosure of my individually identifiable health information or other medical records. This release authority applies to any information governed by the Health Insurance Portability and Accountability Act of 1996 (aka HIPAA), 42 USC 1320d and 45 CFR 160-164.

If I am diagnosed as pregnant, this document shall have no force and effect during my pregnancy.

I understand the full importance of this declaration, and I am emotionally and mentally competent to make this declaration and Living Will. I also understand that I may revoke this document at any time.

I publish and sign this Living Will and Directive to Physicians, consisting of _____ typewritten pages, on _____, 20_____, and declare that I do so freely, for the purposes expressed, under no constraint or undue influence, and that I am of sound mind and of legal age.

_____
Declarant's Signature

_____
Printed Name of Declarant

Witness Attestation

On _____, 20_____, in the presence of all of us, the above-named Declarant published and signed this Living Will and Directive to Physicians, and then at the Declarant's request, and in the Declarant's presence, and in each other's presence, we all signed below as witnesses, and we each declare, under penalty of perjury, that, to the best of our knowledge:

1. The Declarant is personally known to me and, to the best of my knowledge, the Declarant signed this instrument freely, under no constraint or undue influence, and is of sound mind and memory and legal age, and fully aware of the possible consequences of this action.

2. I am at least 19 years of age and I am not related to the Declarant in any manner: by blood, marriage, or adoption.

3. I am not the Declarant's attending physician, or a patient or employee of the Declarant's attending physician; or a patient, physician, or employee of the health care facility in which the Declarant is a patient, unless such person is required or allowed to witness the execution of this document by the laws of the state in which this document is executed.

4. I am not entitled to any portion of the Declarant's estate on the Declarant's death under the laws of intestate succession of any state or country, nor under the Last Will and Testament of the Declarant or any Codicil to such Last Will and Testament.

5. I have no claim against any portion of the Declarant's estate on the Declarant's death.

6. I am not directly financially responsible for the Declarant's medical care.

7. I did not sign the Declarant's signature for the Declarant or on the direction of the Declarant, nor have I been paid any fee for acting as a witness to the execution of this document.

_____
Signature of Witness #1

_____
Printed name of Witness #1

_____
Address of Witness #1

_____
Signature of Witness #2

_____
Printed name of Witness #2

_____
Address of Witness #2

_____
Signature of Witness #3

_____
Printed name of Witness #3

_____
Address of Witness #3

Notary Acknowledgement

County of _____
State of _____

On _____, 20____, before me personally appeared _____, the Declarant, and _____, the first witness, _____, the second witness, _____, the third witness, and, being first sworn on oath and under penalty of perjury, state that, in the presence of all the witnesses, the Declarant published and signed the above Living Will Declaration and Directive to Physicians, and then, at Declarant's request, and in the presence of the Declarant and of each other, each of the witnesses signed as witnesses, and stated that, to the best of their knowledge, the Declarant signed said Living Will Declaration and Directive to Physicians freely, under no constraint or undue influence, and is of sound mind and memory and legal age and fully aware of the potential consequences of this action. The witnesses further state that this affidavit is made at the direction of and in the presence of the Declarant.

_____
Signature of Notary Public

_____
Printed name of Notary Public

Notary Public,
In and for the County of _____
State of _____
My commission expires: _____   Notary Seal

Revocation of Living Will

I, _____ , am the Declarant and maker of a Living Will and Directive to Physicians, dated _____ , 20_____ .

By this written revocation, I hereby entirely revoke such Living Will and Directive to Physicians and intend that it no longer have any force or effect whatsoever.

Dated _____ , 20_____ .

_____
Declarant's Signature

_____
Printed Name of Declarant

_____
Signature of Witness #1

_____
Printed name of Witness #1

_____
Address of Witness #1

_____
Signature of Witness #2

_____
Printed name of Witness #2

_____
Address of Witness #2

Living Trust of _____

Declaration of Trust

I, _____ , the Grantor of this trust,
declare and make this Living Trust on _____ , 20 _____ .

This trust will be known as the _____ Living Trust.

I, _____ , will be Trustee of this trust.

My marital status is that _____ .

Property Transfer

I transfer ownership to this trust of all of the assets that are listed on the attached Schedule of Assets of Living Trust, which is specifically made a part of this trust. I reserve the right to add or delete any of these assets at any time. In addition, I will prepare a separate Deed, Assignment, or any other documents necessary to carry out such transfers. Any additions or deletions to the Schedule of Assets of Living Trust must be written, notarized, and attached to this document to be valid.

Grantor's Rights

Until I die, I retain all rights to all income, profits, and control of the trust property. If my principal residence is transferred to this trust, I retain the right to possess and occupy it for my life, rent-free and without charge. I will remain liable for all taxes, insurance, maintenance, related costs, and expenses. The rights that I retain are intended to give me a beneficial interest in my principal residence such that I do not lose any eligibility that I may have for a state homestead exemption for which I am otherwise qualified.

Successor Trustee

Upon my death or if it is certified by a licensed physician that I am physically or mentally unable to manage this trust and my financial affairs, then I appoint
_____ ,
address:

as Successor Trustee, to serve without bond and without compensation. If this Successor Trustee is not surviving or otherwise unable to serve, I appoint
_____ ,
address:

as Alternate Successor Trustee, also to serve without bond and without compensation. The Successor Trustee or Alternative Successor Trustee shall not be liable for any actions taken in good faith. References to "Trustee" in this document shall include any Successor or Alternative Successor Trustees.

Trustee's Powers

In addition to any powers, authority, and discretion granted by law, I grant the Trustee any and all powers to perform any acts, in his or her sole discretion and without court approval, for the management and distribution of this trust. I intend the Trustee to have the same power and authority to manage and distribute the trust assets as an individual owner has over his or her own wholly owned property.

Additional Trustee Powers

The Trustee's powers include, but are not limited to: the power to sell trust property, borrow money, and encumber that property, specifically including trust real estate, by mortgage, deed of trust, or other method; the power to manage trust real estate as if the Trustee were the absolute owner of it, including the power to lease or grant options to lease the property, make repairs or alterations, and insure against loss; the power to sell or grant options for the sale or exchange of any trust property, including stocks, bonds, and any other form of security; the power to invest trust property in property of any kind, including but not limited to bonds, notes, mortgages, and stocks; the power to receive additional property from any source and add to any trust created by this trust; the power to employ and pay reasonable fees to accountants, lawyers, or investment consultants for information or advice relating to the trust; the power to deposit and hold trust funds in both interest-bearing and non-interest-bearing accounts; the power to deposit funds in a bank or other accounts uninsured by FDIC coverage; the power to enter into electronic funds transfer or safe deposit arrangements with financial institutions; the power to continue any business of the Grantor; and the power to institute or defend legal actions concerning the trust or Grantor's affairs.

Incapacitation

Should the Successor Trustee or Alternative Successor Trustee assume management of this trust during the lifetime of the Grantor, the Successor Trustee or Alternative Successor Trustee shall manage the trust solely for the proper healthcare, support, maintenance, comfort, and/or welfare of the Grantor, in accordance with the Grantor's accustomed manner of living.

Termination of Trust

Upon my death, this trust shall become irrevocable. The Successor Trustee shall then pay my valid debts, last expenses, and estate taxes from the assets of this trust. The Successor Trustee shall then distribute the remaining trust assets in the manner shown on the attached Schedule of Beneficiaries of Living Trust which is specifically made a part of this trust. Any additions or deletions to the Schedule of Beneficiaries of Living Trust must be written, notarized, and attached to this document to be valid.

Survivorship

All beneficiaries named in the Schedule of Beneficiaries of Living Trust must survive me by thirty (30) days to receive any gift under this living trust. If any beneficiary and I should die simultaneously, I shall be conclusively presumed to have survived that beneficiary for purposes of this living trust.

Amendments and Revocations

I reserve the right to amend any or all of this trust at any time. The amendments must be written, notarized, and attached to this document to be valid. I also reserve the right to revoke this trust at any time. A revocation of this trust must be written, notarized, and attached to this document to be valid.

Governing Law

This trust, containing _____ typewritten pages, was created on the date noted above and will be governed under the laws of the State of _____ .

Signature

_____   _____
Signature of Grantor   Printed Name of Grantor

Notary Acknowledgment

State of _____
County of _____

On _____ , 20 ____ , _____
came before me personally and, under oath, stated that he or she is the person described in the above document and he or she signed the above document in my presence. I declare under penalty of perjury that the person whose name is subscribed to this instrument appears to be of sound mind and under no duress, fraud, or undue influence.

_____
Signature of Notary Public

Notary Public, In and for the County of _____
State of _____

My commission expires: _____   Notary Seal

Schedule of Assets of Living Trust

This Schedule of Assets of Living Trust is made on _____ , 20 _____ ,
by _____ , the Grantor, to the
_____ Living Trust dated
_____ , 20 _____ .

All Grantor's right, title, and interest in the following property shall be the property of the trust:

_____ _____
Signature of Grantor   Printed Name of Grantor

Notary Acknowledgment

State of _____
County of _____

On _____ , 20 _____ , _____
came before me personally and, under oath, stated that he or she is the person described in the above document and he or she signed the above document in my presence. I declare under penalty of perjury that the person whose name is subscribed to this instrument appears to be of sound mind and under no duress, fraud, or undue influence.

_____
Signature of Notary Public

Notary Public, In and for the County of _____
State of _____

My commission expires: _____   Notary Seal

Schedule of Beneficiaries of Living Trust

This Schedule of Beneficiaries is made on _____ , 20 _____ , by _____ , the Grantor, to the _____ Living Trust dated _____ .

Upon the death of the Grantor of the trust and the payment of all debts, taxes, and liabilities of the Grantor, the Successor Trustee shall distribute the remaining assets of the Trust as follows:

To _____ ,
address:

my _____ , or if not surviving, to _____ ,
address:

my _____ , the following trust assets shall be distributed:

All the rest and residue of the trust assets shall be distributed to
_____ ,
address:

my _____ , or if not surviving, to
_____ ,
address:

my _____ .

If any of the beneficiaries named on this Schedule of Beneficiaries is subject to the terms of any children's trust in the main trust document to which this Schedule pertains, then any property distributed to such beneficiary shall be subject to the terms of any such children's trust.

_____
Signature of Grantor

_____
Printed Name of Grantor

Notary Acknowledgment

State of _____
County of _____

On _____ , 20 _____ , _____
came before me personally and, under oath, stated that he or she is the person described in the above document and he or she signed the above document in my presence. I declare under penalty of perjury that the person whose name is subscribed to this instrument appears to be of sound mind and under no duress, fraud, or undue influence.

_____
Signature of Notary Public

Notary Public, In and for the County of _____
State of _____

My commission expires: _____   Notary Seal

Assignment to Living Trust

This Assignment to Living Trust is made on _____ , 20 _____ , between
_____ , the Grantor, and the
_____ Living Trust dated
_____ , 20 _____ .

The Grantor transfers and conveys possession, ownership, and all right, title, and interest in the following property to the Living Trust:

The Grantor warrants that he or she owns this property and that he or she has the full authority to transfer and convey the property to the Living Trust. Grantor also warrants that the property is transferred free and clear of all liens, indebtedness, or liabilities.

Signed and delivered to the Living Trust on the above date.

_____   _____
Signature of Grantor   Printed Name of Grantor

Notary Acknowledgment

State of _____
County of _____

On _____ , 20 _____ , _____
came before me personally and, under oath, stated that he or she is the person described in the above document and he or she signed the above document in my presence. I declare under penalty of perjury that the person whose name is subscribed to this instrument appears to be of sound mind and under no duress, fraud, or undue influence.

_____
Signature of Notary Public

Notary Public, In and for the County of _____
State of _____

My commission expires: _____   Notary Seal

Amendment of Living Trust

This Amendment of Living Trust is made on _____ , 20 _____ , by
_____ , the Grantor, to the
_____ Living Trust dated
_____ , 20 _____ .

The Grantor modifies the original trust as follows:

All other terms and conditions of the original Living Trust remain in effect without modification. This Amendment, including the original Living Trust, is the entire Living Trust as of this date. The Grantor has signed this Amendment on the date specified at the beginning of this Amendment.

_____   _____
Signature of Grantor   Printed Name of Grantor

Notary Acknowledgment

State of _____
County of _____

On _____ , 20 _____ , _____
came before me personally and, under oath, stated that he or she is the person described in the above document and he or she signed the above document in my presence. I declare under penalty of perjury that the person whose name is subscribed to this instrument appears to be of sound mind and under no duress, fraud, or undue influence.

_____
Signature of Notary Public

Notary Public, In and for the County of _____
State of _____

My commission expires: _____   Notary Seal

Revocation of Living Trust

On this date _____ , 20 _____ ,
I, _____ , the Grantor, fully and completely revoke the _____ Living Trust dated _____ , 20 _____ . All property that is held in trust shall be returned to the Grantor as my sole property.

_____
Signature of Grantor

_____
Printed Name of Grantor

Notary Acknowledgment

State of _____
County of _____

On _____ , 20 _____ , _____
came before me personally and, under oath, stated that he or she is the person described in the above document and he or she signed the above document in my presence. I declare under penalty of perjury that the person whose name is subscribed to this instrument appears to be of sound mind and under no duress, fraud, or undue influence.

_____
Signature of Notary Public

Notary Public, In and for the County of _____
State of _____

My commission expires: _____   Notary Seal

General Release

For consideration, I, _____,
address:

release _____,
address:

from all claims and obligations, known or unknown, to this date arising from the following transaction or incident:

The party signing this release has not assigned any claims or obligations covered by this release to any other party.

The party signing this release intends that it both bind and benefit itself and any successors.

Dated _____, 20 _____

_____
Signature

_____
Printed Name

Mutual Release

For consideration, _____,
address:

and _____,
address:

release each other from all claims and obligations, known or unknown, that they may have against each other arising from the following transaction or incident:

Neither party has assigned any claims or obligations covered by this release to any other party.

Both parties signing this release intend that it both bind and benefit themselves and any successors.

Dated _____, 20 _____

_____ _____
Signature   Signature

_____ _____
Printed Name   Printed Name

Specific Release

For consideration, I, _____,
address:

release _____,
address:

from the following specific claims and obligations:

arising from the following transaction or incident:

Any claims or obligations that are not specifically mentioned are not released by this Specific Release.

The party signing this release has not assigned any claims or obligations covered by this release to any other party.

The party signing this release intends that it both bind and benefit itself and any successors.

Dated _____, 20 _____

_____
Signature

_____
Printed Name

Receipt in Full

The undersigned acknowledges receipt of the sum of $ _____ paid by
_____ .

This payment constitutes full payment and satisfaction of the following obligation:

Dated _____ , 20 _____

_____
Signature of Person Receiving Payment

_____
Printed Name of Person Receiving Payment

Receipt on Account

The undersigned acknowledges receipt of the sum of $ _____ paid by
_____ .

This payment will be applied and credited to the following account:

Dated _____ , 20 _____

_____
Signature of Person Receiving Payment

_____
Printed Name of Person Receiving Payment

Receipt for Goods

The undersigned acknowledges receipt of the goods which are described on the attached purchase order. The undersigned also acknowledges that these goods have been inspected and found to be in conformance with the purchase order specifications.

Dated _____ , 20 _____

_____
Signature of Person Receiving Goods

_____
Printed Name of Person Receiving Goods

Residential Lease

This lease is made on _____ , 20 _____ , between
_____ , landlord,
address: _____
and _____ , tenant,
address: _____

1. The landlord agrees to rent to the tenant and the tenant agrees to rent from the landlord the following residence:

2. The term of this lease will be from _____ , 20 _____ , until _____
_____ , 20 _____ .

3. The rental payments will be $ _____ per _____ and will be payable by the tenant to the landlord on the { _____ day of each month, beginning on _____ , 20 _____ .

4. The tenant has paid the landlord a security deposit of $ _____ . This security deposit will be held as security for the repair of any damages to the residence by the tenant. This deposit will be returned to the tenant within ten (10) days of the termination of this lease, minus any amounts needed to repair the residence, but without interest, except as required by law in the State of _____ .

5. The Tenant has paid the Landlord an additional month's rent in the amount of $ _____
_____ . This rent deposit will be held as security for the payment of rent by the tenant. This rent payment deposit will be returned to the tenant within ten (10) days of the termination of this lease, minus any rent still due upon termination but without interest, except as required by law in the State of _____ .

6. Tenant agrees to maintain the residence in a clean and sanitary manner and not to make any alterations to the residence without the landlord's written consent. Tenant also agrees not to conduct any business in the residence. At the termination of this lease, the tenant agrees to leave the residence in the same condition as when it was received, except for normal wear and tear.

7. Tenant also agrees not to conduct any type of business in the residence,

nor store or use any dangerous or hazardous materials. Tenant agrees that the residence is to be used only as a single family residence, with a maximum of _____ tenants. Tenant also agrees to comply with all rules, laws, and ordinances affecting the residence, including all laws of the State of t_____. Tenant agrees that no pets or other animals are allowed in the residence without the written permission of the Landlord.

8. The landlord agrees to supply the following utilities to the tenant:

9. The tenant agrees to obtain and pay for the following utilities:

10. Tenant agrees not to sublet the residence or assign this lease without the landlord's written consent. Tenant agrees to allow the landlord reasonable access to the residence for inspection and repair. Landlord agrees to enter the residence only after notifying the tenant in advance, except in an emergency, and according to the laws of the State of _____.

11. The tenant has inspected the residence and has found it satisfactory.

12. If the tenant fails to pay the rent on time or violates any other terms of this lease, the landlord will have the right to terminate this lease in accordance with state law. The landlord will also have the right to re-enter the residence and take possession of it and to take advantage of any other legal remedies available under the laws of the State of _____.

13. If the Tenant remains as tenant after the expiration of this lease without signing a new lease, a month-to-month tenancy will be created with the same terms and conditions as this lease, except that such new tenancy may be terminated by thirty (30) days written notice from either the Tenant or the Landlord.

14. As required by law, the landlord makes the following statement: "Radon gas is a naturally occurring radioactive gas that, when accumulated in sufficient quantities in a building, may present health risks to persons exposed to it. Levels of radon gas that exceed federal and state guidelines have been found in buildings in this state. Additional information regarding radon gas and radon gas testing may be obtained from your county health department."

15. As required by law, the landlord makes the following LEAD WARNING STATEMENT:

"Every purchaser or lessee of any interest in residential real property on which a residential dwelling was built prior to 1978 is notified that such property may present exposure to lead from lead-based paint that may place young children at risk of developing lead poisoning. Lead poisoning in young children may produce permanent neurological damage, including learning disabilities, reduced intelligence quotient, behavioral problems, and impaired memory. Lead poisoning also poses a particular threat to pregnant women. The seller or lessor of any interest in residential real estate is required to provide the buyer with any information on lead-based paint hazards from risk assessments or inspection in the seller's or lessor's possession and notify the buyer or lessee of any known lead-based paint hazards. A risk assessment or inspection for possible lead-based paint hazards is recommended prior to purchase."

Landlord's Disclosure
Presence of lead-based paint and/or lead-based paint hazards: (Landlord to initial one).o

_____ Known lead-based paint and/or lead-based paint hazards are present in building (explain):
_____ Landlord has no knowledge of lead-based paint and/or lead-based paint hazards in building.
Records and reports available to landlord: (Landlord to initial one). p
_____ Landlord has provided tenant with all available records and reports pertaining to lead-based paint and/or lead-based paint hazards are present in building (list documents):
_____ Landlord has no records and reports pertaining to lead-based paint and/or lead-based paint hazards in building.

Tenant's Acknowledgment
(Tenant to initial all applicable).

_____ Tenant has received copies of all information listed above.
_____ Tenant has received the pamphlet "Protect Your Family from Lead in Your Home."
_____ Tenant has received a ten (10)-day opportunity (or mutually agreed on period) to conduct a risk assessment or inspection for the presence of lead-based paint and/or lead-based paint hazards in building.
_____ Tenant has waived the opportunity to conduct a risk assessment or inspection for the presence of lead-based paint and/or lead-based paint hazards in building.

The landlord and tenant have reviewed the information above and certify, by their signatures at the end of this lease, to the best of their knowledge, that the information they have provided is true and accurate.

16. The following are additional terms of this lease:

17. The parties agree that this lease is the entire agreement between them. This lease binds and benefits both the landlord and tenant and any successors. This Lease is governed by the laws of the State of _____ .

_____ _____
Signature of Landlord   Signature of Tenant

_____ _____
Printed Name of Landlord   Printed Name of Tenant

Month to Month Rental Agreement

This Agreement is made on _____ , 20 _____ , between
_____ , landlord,
address:

and _____ , tenant,
address:

1. The Landlord agrees to rent to the Tenant and the Tenant agrees to rent from the Landlord on a month-to-month basis, the following residence:

2. This Agreement will begin on _____ and will continue on a month-to-month basis until terminated. This agreement may only be terminated by _____ days written notice from either party.

3. The rental payments will be $ _____ per _____ and will be payable by the tenant to the landlord on the _____ day of each month, beginning on _____ , 20 _____ .

4. The tenant has paid the landlord a security deposit of $ _____ . This security deposit will be held as security for the repair of any damages to the residence by the tenant. This deposit will be returned to the tenant within ten (10) days of the termination of this agreement, minus any amounts needed to repair the residence, but without interest, except as required by law in the State of __ _____ .

5. The Tenant has paid the Landlord an additional month's rent in the amount of $ _____ . This rent deposit will be held as security for the payment of rent by the tenant. This rent payment deposit will be returned to the tenant within ten (10) days of the termination of this agreement, minus any rent still due upon termination but without interest, except as required by law in the State of _____ .

6. Tenant agrees to maintain the residence in a clean and sanitary manner and not to make any alterations to the residence without the landlord's written consent. Tenant also agrees not to conduct any business in the residence. At the termination of this agreement, the tenant agrees to leave the residence in the same condition as when it was received, except for normal wear and tear.

7. Tenant also agrees not to conduct any type of business in the residence, nor store or use any dangerous or hazardous materials. Tenant agrees that the residence is to be used only as a single family residence, with a maximum of _____ tenants. Tenant also agrees to comply with all rules, laws, and ordinances affecting the residence, including all the laws of the State of _____. Tenant agrees that no pets or other animals are allowed in the residence without the written permission of the Landlord.

8. The landlord agrees to supply the following utilities to the tenant:

9. The tenant agrees to obtain and pay for the following utilities:

10. Tenant agrees not to sublet the residence or assign this agreement without the landlord's written consent. Tenant agrees to allow the landlord reasonable access to the residence for inspection and repair. Landlord agrees to enter the residence only after notifying the tenant in advance, except in an emergency, and according to the laws of the State of _____.

11. The tenant has inspected the residence and has found it satisfactory.

12. If the tenant fails to pay the rent on time or violates any other terms of this agreement, the landlord will have the right to terminate this agreement in accordance with state law. The landlord will also have the right to re-enter the residence and take possession of it and to take advantage of any other legal remedies available.

13. As required by law, the landlord makes the following statement: "Radon gas is a naturally occurring radioactive gas that, when accumulated in sufficient quantities in a building, may present health risks to persons exposed to it. Levels of radon gas that exceed federal and state guidelines have been found in buildings in this state. Additional information regarding radon gas and radon gas testing may be obtained from your county health department."

14. As required by law, the landlord makes the following **LEAD WARNING STATEMENT**: "Every purchaser or lessee of any interest in residential real property on which a residential dwelling was built prior to 1978 is notified that such property may present exposure to lead from lead-based paint that may place young children at risk of developing lead poisoning. Lead poisoning in young children may produce permanent neurological damage, including learning disabilities, reduced intelligence quotient, behavioral problems, and impaired memory. Lead poisoning also poses a particular threat to pregnant women. The seller or lessor of any interest in residential real estate is required to provide the buyer or lessee with any information on lead-based paint hazards from risk assessments or inspection in the seller's or lessor's possession and notify the buyer or lessee of any known lead-based paint hazards. A risk assessment or inspection for possible lead-based paint hazards is recommended prior to purchase."

Landlord's Disclosure

Presence of lead-based paint and/or lead-based paint hazards: (Landlord to initial one).

_____ Known lead-based paint and/or lead-based paint hazards are present in building (explain):

_____ Landlord has no knowledge of lead-based paint and/or lead-based paint hazards in building.

Records and reports available to landlord: (Landlord to initial one).

_____ Landlord has provided tenant with all available records and reports pertaining to lead-based paint and/or lead-based paint hazards are present in building (list documents):

_____ Landlord has no records and reports pertaining to lead-based paint and/or lead-based paint hazards in building.

Tenant's Acknowledgment

(Tenant to initial all applicable).

_____ Tenant has received copies of all information listed above.

_____ Tenant has received the pamphlet "Protect Your Family from Lead in Your Home."

_____ Tenant has received a ten (10)-day opportunity (or mutually agreed on period) to conduct a risk assessment or inspection for the presence of lead-based paint and/or lead-based paint hazards in building.

_____ Tenant has waived the opportunity to conduct a risk assessment or inspection for the presence of lead-based paint and/or lead-based paint hazards in building.

The landlord and tenant have reviewed the information above and certify, by their signatures at the end of this agreement, to the best of their knowledge, that the information they have provided is true and accurate.

15. The following are additional terms of this agreement:

16. The parties agree that this agreement is the entire agreement between them. This Agreement binds and benefits both the landlord and tenant and any successors. This Agreement is governed by the laws of the State of _____ .

_____   _____
Signature of Landlord   Signature of Tenant

_____   _____
Printed Name of Landlord   Printed Name of Tenant

Amendment of Lease

This Amendment of Lease is made on _____ , 20 ____ , between
_____ , Landlord,
address:

and _____ , Tenant,
address:

For valuable consideration, the parties agree as follows:

1. The following described lease is attached to this amendment and is made a part of this amendment:

2. The parties agree to amend this lease as follows:

3. All other terms and conditions of the original lease remain in effect without modification. This amendment binds and benefits both parties and any successors. This document, including the attached lease, is the entire agreement between the parties.

The parties have signed this amendment on the date specified at the beginning of this amendment.

_____   _____
Signature of Landlord   Signature of Tenant

_____   _____
Printed Name of Landlord   Printed Name of Tenant

Extension of Lease

This Extension of Lease is made on _____ , 20 _____ , between
_____ , Landlord,
address:

and _____ , Tenant,
address:

For valuable consideration, the parties agree as follows:

1. The following described lease will end on _____ , 20 _____ :

   This lease is attached to this extension and is a part of this extension.

2. The parties agree to extend this lease for an additional period, which will begin immediately on the expiration of the original time period and will end on
_____ , 20 ____ .

3. The extension of this lease will be on the same terms and conditions as the original lease. This extension binds and benefits both parties and any successors. This document, including the attached lease, is the entire agreement between the parties.

The parties have signed this extension on the date specified at the beginning of this extension.

_____   _____
Signature of Landlord   Signature of Tenant

_____   _____
Printed Name of Landlord   Printed Name of Tenant

Sublease

This Sublease is made on _____ , 20 _____ , between
_____ , Tenant,
address:

and _____ , Subtenant,
address:

For valuable consideration, the parties agree to the following terms and conditions:

1. The Tenant subleases to the Subtenant the following described property:

2. This property is currently leased to the Tenant under the terms of the following described lease:

   This lease is attached to this sublease and is a part of this sublease.

3. This sublease will be for the period from _____ , 20 _____ ,
   to _____ , 20 _____ .

4. The subrental payments will be $ _____ per _____ and will be payable by the Subtenant to the Landlord on the _____ day of each month, beginning on _____ , 20 _____ .

5. The Tenant warrants that the underlying lease is in effect, has not been modified, and that the property may be sublet. If the consent of the Landlord is necessary for this sublease to be effective, such consent is attached to this sublease and is a part of this sublease. Tenant agrees to indemnify and hold the Subtenant harmless from any claim which may result from the Tenant's failure to perform under this lease prior to the date of this sublease.

6. The Subtenant agrees to perform all of the obligations of the Tenant under the original lease and receive all of the benefits of the Tenant under this lease. Subtenant agrees to indemnify and hold the Tenant harmless from any claim which may result from the Subtenant's failure to perform under this lease after the date of this sublease.

7. The Tenant agrees to remain primarily liable to the Landlord for the obligations under the lease.

8. The parties agree to the following additional terms:

9. This sublease binds and benefits both parties and any successors. This sublease, including any attachments, is the entire agreement between the parties.

_____ _____
Signature of Tenant   Signature of Subtenant

_____ _____
Printed Name of Tenant   Printed Name of Subtenant

Consent to Sublease of Lease

Date: _____ , 20 _____

To: _____

I am the Landlord under the following described lease:

This lease is the subject of the attached sublease.

I consent to the sublease of this lease as described in the attached sublease, which provides that the Subtenant is substituted for the Tenant for the period indicated in the sublease. This consent does not release the Tenant from any obligations under the lease and the Tenant remains fully bound under the lease.

_____
Signature of Landlord

_____
Printed Name of Landlord

Notice of Breach of Lease

Date: _____ , 20 _____

To: _____

RE: Breach of Lease

Dear _____ :

This notice is in reference to the following described lease:

Please be advised that as of _____ , 20 _____ , we are holding you in BREACH OF LEASE for the following reasons:

If this breach of lease is not corrected within _____ days of this notice, we will take further action to protect our rights, which may include termination of this lease. This notice is made under all applicable laws. All of our rights are reserved under this notice.

_____
Signature

_____
Printed Name

Notice of Rent Default

Date: _____, 20 _____

To: _____

RE: Rent Default

Dear _____ :

This notice is in reference to the following described lease:

Please be advised that as of _____, 20 _____ , you are in DEFAULT IN YOUR PAYMENT OF RENT in the amount of $ _____ .

If this breach of lease is not corrected within _____ days of this notice, we will take further action to protect our rights, which may include termination of this lease and collection proceedings. This notice is made under all applicable laws. All of our rights are reserved under this notice.

_____
Signature of Landlord

_____
Printed Name of Landlord

Notice to Vacate Property

Date: _____ , 20 _____

To: _____

RE: Vacate Property

Dear _____ :

This notice is in reference to the following described lease:

Please be advised that since _____ , 20 _____ , you have been in BREACH OF LEASE for the following reasons:

You were previously notified of this breach in the NOTICE dated _____ , 20 _____ . At that time you were given _____ days to correct the breach of the lease and you have not complied.

THEREFORE, YOU ARE HEREBY GIVEN NOTICE:

To immediately vacate the property and deliver possession to the Landlord on or before _____ , 20 _____ . If you fail to correct the breach of lease or vacate the property by this date, legal action to evict you from the property will be taken. Regardless of your vacating the property, you are still responsible for all rent due under the lease.

_____
Signature of Landlord

_____
Printed Name of Landlord

Notice to Terminate Lease

Date: _____ , 20 _____

To: _____

RE: Terminate Lease

Dear _____ :

This notice is in reference to the following described lease:

Please be advised that as of _____ , 20 _____ , you have been in BREACH OF LEASE for the following reasons:

You were previously notified of this breach in the NOTICE dated _____ , 20 _____ . At that time you were given _____ days to correct the breach of the lease and you have not complied.

THEREFORE, YOU ARE HEREBY GIVEN NOTICE:

The lease is immediately terminated. Possession of the property to the Landlord will take place on or before _____ , 20 _____ .

_____
Signature

_____
Printed Name

Receipt for Lease Security Deposit

The Landlord acknowledges receipt of the sum of $ _____ paid by the Tenant under the following described lease:

This security deposit payment will be held by the Landlord under the terms of this lease, and unless required by law, will not bear any interest. This security deposit will be repaid when due under the terms of the lease.

Dated: _____ , 20 _____

_____
Signature of Landlord

_____
Printed Name of Landlord

Rent Receipt

The Landlord acknowledges receipt of the sum of $ _____ paid by
_____ , the Tenant.
This payment will be applied and credited to the rent due for the period of
_____ , 20 _____ , on the following described property:

Dated: _____ , 20 _____

_____
Signature of Landlord

_____
Printed Name of Landlord

Personal Property Rental Agreement

This Agreement is made on _____, 20 _____, between
_____, Owner,
address:

and _____, Renter,
address:

1. The Owner agrees to rent to the Renter and the Renter agrees to rent from the Owner the following property:

2. The term of this agreement will be from _____ o'clock ____ . m., _____, 20 _____, until _____ o'clock ____ . m., _____, 20 _____ .

3. The rental payments will be $ _____ per _____ and will be payable by the Renter to the Owner as follows:

4. This agreement may be terminated by either party by giving twenty-four (24) hours notice to the other party.

5. The parties agree that this agreement is the entire agreement between them. This agreement binds and benefits both the Owner and Renter and any successors.

_____   _____
Signature of Owner   Signature of Renter

_____   _____
Printed Name of Owner   Printed Name of Renter

Contract for Sale of Personal Property

This Contract is made on _____ , 20 _____ , between
_____ , Seller,
address:

and _____ , Buyer,
address:

1. The Seller agrees to sell to the Buyer, and the Buyer agrees to buy the following personal property:

2. The Buyer agrees to pay the Seller $ _____ for the property. The Buyer agrees to pay this purchase price in the following manner:

3. The Buyer will be entitled to possession of this property on _____ , 20 _____ .

4. The Seller represents that it has legal title to the property and full authority to sell the property. Seller also represents that the property is sold free and clear of all liens, indebtedness, or liabilities. Seller agrees to provide Buyer with a Bill of Sale for the property.

5. This Contract binds and benefits both the Buyer and Seller and any successors. This document, including any attachments, is the entire agreement between the Buyer and Seller. This agreement is governed by the laws of the State of _____ .

_____   _____
Signature of Seller   Signature of Buyer

_____   _____
Printed Name of Seller   Printed Name of Buyer

Bill of Sale, with Warranties

This Bill of Sale is made on _____ , 20 _____ , between
_____ , Seller,
address:

and _____ , Buyer,
address:

In exchange for the payment of $ _____ , received from the Buyer, the Seller sells and transfers possession of the following property to the Buyer:

The Seller warrants that it owns this property and that it has the authority to sell the property to the Buyer. Seller also warrants that the property is sold free and clear of all liens, indebtedness, or liabilities.

The Seller also warrants that the property is in good working condition as of this date.

Signed and delivered to the Buyer on the above date.

_____
Signature of Seller

_____
Printed Name of Seller

Bill of Sale, with Warranties

This Bill of Sale is made on _____ , 20 _____ , between
_____ , Seller,
address:

and _____ , Buyer,
address:

In exchange for the payment of $ _____ , received from the Buyer, the Seller sells and transfers possession of the following property to the Buyer:

The Seller warrants that it owns this property and that it has the authority to sell the property to the Buyer. Seller also warrants that the property is sold free and clear of all liens, indebtedness, or liabilities.

The Seller also warrants that the property is in good working condition as of this date.

Signed and delivered to the Buyer on the above date.

_____
Signature of Seller

_____
Printed Name of Seller

Bill of Sale, without Warranties

This Bill of Sale is made on _____ , 20 _____ , between
_____ , Seller,
address:

and _____ , Buyer,
address:

In exchange for the payment of $ _____ , received from the Buyer, the Seller sells and transfers possession of the following property to the Buyer:

The Seller disclaims any implied warranty of merchantability or fitness and the property is sold in its present condition, "as is."

Signed and delivered to the Buyer on the above date.

_____
Signature of Seller

_____
Printed Name of Seller

Bill of Sale, Subject to Debt

This Bill of Sale is made on _____ , 20 _____ , between
_____ , Seller,
address:

and _____ , Buyer,
address:

In exchange for the payment of $ _____ , received from the Buyer, the Seller sells and transfers possession of the following property to the Buyer:

The Seller warrants that it owns this property and that it has the authority to sell the property to the Buyer. Seller also states that the property is sold subject to the following debt:

The Buyer buys the property subject to the above debt and agrees to pay the debt. Buyer also agrees to indemnify and hold the Seller harmless from any claim based on failure to pay off this debt.

The Seller also warrants that the property is in good working condition as of this date.

Signed and delivered to the Buyer on the above date.

_____   _____
Signature of Seller   Signature of Buyer

_____   _____
Printed Name of Seller   Printed Name of Buyer

Agreement to Sell Real Estate

This agreement is made on _____ , 20 _____ , between
_____ , seller,
address:

and _____ , buyer,
address:

The seller now owns the following described real estate, located at
_____ ,
City of _____ , State of _____ , and legally described as follows:

For valuable consideration, the seller agrees to sell and the buyer agrees to buy this property for the following price and on the following terms:

1. The seller will sell this property to the buyer, free from all claims, liabilities, and indebtedness, unless noted in this agreement.

2. The following personal property is also included in this sale:

3. The buyer agrees to pay the seller the sum of $ _____ , which the seller agrees to accept as full payment. This agreement, however, is conditional upon the buyer being able to arrange suitable financing on the following terms at least thirty (30) days prior to the closing date for this agreement: A mortgage in the amount of $ _____ , payable in _____ monthly payments, with an annual interest rate of _____ % (_____ percent) .

4. The purchase price will be paid as follows:
   Earnest deposit .... $ _____
   Other deposit: .... $ _____
   Cash or certified check on closing .... $ _____
   (subject to any adjustments or prorations on closing)
   Total Purchase Price .... $ _____

5. The seller acknowledges receiving the earnest money deposit of $ _____ from the buyer. If buyer fails to perform this agreement, the seller shall retain this money.
   If seller fails to perform this agreement, this money shall be returned to the buyer or the buyer may have the right of specific performance. If buyer is unable to obtain suitable financing at least thirty (30) days prior to closing, then this money will be returned to the buyer without penalty or interest.

6. This agreement will close on _____ , 20 _____ , at _____ o'clock ____ . m., at _____ , City of _____ , State of _____ . At that time, and upon payment by the buyer of the portion of the purchase price then due, the seller will deliver to buyer the following documents:

(a) A Bill of Sale for all personal property
(b) A Warranty Deed for the real estate
(c) A Seller's Affidavit of Title
(d) A closing statement
(e) Other documents:

7. At closing, pro-rated adjustments to the purchase price will be made for the following items:
(a) Utilities
(b) Property taxes
(c) The following other items:

8. The following closing costs will be paid by the seller:

9. The following closing costs will be paid by the buyer:

10. Seller represents that it has good and marketable title to the property and will supply the buyer with either an abstract of title or a standard policy of title insurance. Seller further represents that the property is free and clear of any restrictions on transfer, claims, indebtedness, or liabilities except the following:
(a) Zoning, restrictions, prohibitions, or requirements imposed by any governmental authority
(b) Any restrictions appearing on the plat of record of the property
(c) Public utility easements of record
(d) Other:

Seller warrants that there shall be no violations of zoning or building codes as of the date of closing. Seller also warrants that all personal property included in this sale will be delivered in working order on the date of closing.

11. At least thirty (30) days prior to closing, buyer shall have the right to obtain a written report from a licensed termite inspector stating that there is no termite infestation or termite damage to the property. If there is such evidence, seller shall remedy such infestation and/or repair such damage, up to a maximum cost of two (2) percent of the purchase price of the property. If the costs exceed two (2) percent of the purchase price and seller elects not to pay for the costs over two (2) percent, buyer may cancel this agreement and the escrow shall be returned to buyer without penalty or interest.

12. At least thirty (30) days prior to closing, buyer or their agent shall have the right to inspect all heating, air conditioning, electrical, and mechanical systems of the property, the roof and all structural components of the property, and any personal property included in this agreement. If any such systems or equipment are not in working order, seller shall pay for the cost of placing them in working order prior to closing. Buyer or their agent may again inspect the property within forty-eight (48) hours of closing to determine if all systems and equipment are in working order.

13. Between the date of this agreement and the date for closing, the property shall be maintained in the condition as existed on the date of this agreement. If there is any damage by fire, casualty, or otherwise, prior to closing, seller shall restore the property to the condition as existed on the date of this agreement. If seller fails to do so, buyer may:

(a) accept the property, as is, along with any insurance proceeds due seller, *or*
(b) cancel this agreement and have the escrow deposit returned, without penalty or interest.

14. As required by law, the seller makes the following statement: "Radon gas is a naturally occurring radioactive gas that, when accumulated in sufficient quantities in a building, may present health risks to persons exposed to it. Levels of radon gas that exceed federal and state guidelines have been found in buildings in this state. Additional information regarding radon gas and radon gas testing may be obtained from your county health department."

15. As required by law, the seller makes the following Lead Warning Statement: "Every purchaser of any interest in residential real property on which a residential dwelling was built prior to 1978 is notified that such property may present exposure to lead from lead-based paint that may place young children at risk of developing lead poisoning. Lead poisoning in young children may produce permanent neurological damage, including learning disabilities, reduced intelligence quotient, behavioral problems, and impaired memory. Lead poisoning also poses a particular threat to pregnant women. The seller of any interest in residential real estate is required to provide the buyer with any information on lead-based paint hazards from risk assessments or inspection in the seller's possession and notify the buyer of any known lead-based paint hazards. A risk assessment or inspection for possible lead-based paint hazards is recommended prior to purchase."

Seller's Disclosure
    Presence of lead-based paint and/or lead-based paint hazards: (Seller to initial one).
    _____ Known lead-based paint and/or lead-based paint hazards are present in building (explain):
    _____ Seller has no knowledge of lead-based paint and/or lead-based paint hazards in building.
    Records and reports available to seller: (Seller to initial one).
    _____ Seller has provided buyer with all available records and reports pertaining to lead-based paint and/or lead-based paint hazards are present in building (list documents):
    _____ Seller has no records and reports pertaining to lead-based paint and/or lead-based paint hazards in building.

Buyer's Acknowledgment
(Buyer to initial all applicable).
    _____ Buyer has received copies of all information listed above.
    _____ Buyer has received the pamphlet "Protect Your Family From Lead in Your Home."
    _____ Buyer has received a ten (10)-day opportunity (or mutually agreed-on period) to conduct a risk assessment or inspection for the presence of lead-based paint and/or lead-based paint hazards in building.
    _____ Buyer has waived the opportunity to conduct a risk assessment or inspection for the presence of lead-based paint and/or lead-based paint hazards in building.

The seller and buyer have reviewed the information above and certify, by their signatures at the end of this agreement, that to the best of their knowledge, the information they have provided is true and accurate.

16. Seller agrees to provide Buyer with a Real Estate Disclosure Statement (or its equivalent that is acceptable in the State in which the property is located) within five (5) days of the signing of this Agreement. Upon receipt of the Real Estate Disclosure Statement from Seller, Buyer shall have

five (5) business days within which to rescind this Agreement by providing Seller with a written and signed statement rescinding this Agreement. The disclosures in the Real Estate Disclosure Statement are made by the seller concerning the condition of the property and are provided on the basis of the seller's actual knowledge of the property on the date of this disclosure. These disclosures are not the representations of any real estate agent or other party. The disclosures themselves are not intended to be a part of any written agreement between the buyer and seller. In addition, the disclosure shall not, in any way, be construed to be a warranty of any kind by the seller.

17. The parties also agree to the following additional terms:

18. No modification of this agreement will be effective unless it is in writing and is signed by both the buyer and seller. This agreement binds and benefits both the buyer and seller and any successors. Time is of the essence of this agreement. This document, including any attachments, is the entire agreement between the buyer and seller. This agreement is governed by the laws of the State of _____ .

_____ _____
Signature of Seller Printed Name of Seller

_____ _____
Signature of Witness for Seller Printed Name of Witness for Seller

_____ _____
Signature of Witness for Seller Printed Name of Witness for Seller

_____ _____
Signature of Buyer Printed Name of Buyer

_____ _____
Signature of Witness for Buyer Printed Name of Witness for Buyer

_____ _____
Signature of Witness for Buyer Printed Name of Witness for Buyer

Option to Buy Real Estate Agreement

This Agreement is made on _____ , 20 _____ , between
_____ , Seller,
address:

and _____ , Buyer,
address:

The Seller now owns the following described real estate, located at
_____ ,
City of _____ , State of _____ :

For valuable consideration, the Seller agrees to give the Buyer an exclusive option to buy this property for the following price and on the following terms:

1. The Buyer will pay the Seller $ _____ for this option. This amount will be credited against the purchase price of the property if this option is exercised by the Buyer. If the option is not exercised, the Seller will retain this payment.

2. The option period will be from the date of this agreement until _____ , 20 _____ , at which time the option provided by this agreement will expire unless exercised.

3. During this period, the Buyer has the option and exclusive right to buy the Seller's property mentioned above for the purchase price of $ _____ . The Buyer must notify the Seller, in writing, of the decision to exercise this option.

4. Attached to this Option to Buy Real Estate Agreement is a completed Contract for the Sale of Real Estate. If the Buyer notifies the Seller, in writing, of the decision to exercise the option within the option period, the Seller and Buyer agree to sign the contract for the sale of real estate and complete the sale on the terms contained in the contract.

5. No modification of this agreement will be effective unless it is in writing and is signed by both the Buyer and Seller. This agreement binds and benefits both the Buyer and Seller and any successors. Time is of the essence of this agreement. This document, including any attachments, is the entire agreement between the Buyer and Seller. This agreement is governed by the laws of the State of _____ .

_____ _____
Signature of Seller   Signature of Buyer

_____ _____
Printed Name of Seller   Printed Name of Buyer

Recording requested by: _____   Space above reserved for use by Recorder's Office
When recorded, mail to: Document prepared by:
Name: _____   Name _____
Address: _____   Address _____
City/State/Zip_____   City/State/Zip _____
Property Tax Parcel/Account Number: _____

Quitclaim Deed

This Quitclaim Deed is made on _____ , between _____ , Grantor, of _____ , City of _____ , State of _____ , and, Grantee, _____ of _____ _____ , City of _____ , State of _____ .

For valuable consideration, the Grantor hereby quitclaims and transfers all right, title, and interest held by the Grantor in the following described real estate and improvements to the Grantee, and his or her heirs and assigns, to have and hold forever, located at _____ _____ City of _____ , State of _____ , and described as follows:

Subject to all easements, rights of way, protective covenants, and mineral reservations of record, if any. Taxes for the tax year of _____ shall be prorated between the Grantor and Grantee as of the date of recording of this deed.

Dated: _____

_____
Signature of Grantor

_____
Name of Grantor

_____   _____
Signature of Witness #1   Printed Name of Witness #1

_____   _____
Signature of Witness #2   Printed Name of Witness #2

State of _____
County of _____

On _____, the Grantor, _____,
personally came before me and, being duly sworn, did state and prove that he/she is the person described in the above document and that he/she signed the above document in my presence.

_____
Notary Signature
Notary Public,
In and for the County of _____ State of _____
My commission expires: _____ Seal

Send all tax statements to Grantee.

Recording requested by: _____   Space above reserved for use by Recorder's Office
When recorded, mail to: Document prepared by:
Name: _____   Name _____
Address: _____   Address _____
City/State/Zip_____   City/State/Zip _____
Property Tax Parcel/Account Number: _____

Warranty Deed

This Warranty Deed is made on _____ , between
_____ , Grantor, of _____
_____ , City of _____ , State of _____ , and, Grantee, _____
_____ of _____ , City of _____ , State of _____ .

For valuable consideration, the Grantor hereby sells, grants, and conveys the following described real estate, in fee simple, to the Grantee to have and hold forever, along with all easements, rights, and buildings belonging to the described property, located at ____ _____ , City of _____ , State of _____ ; legally described as follows:

The Grantor warrants that it is lawful owner and has full right to convey the property, and that the property is free from all claims, liabilities, or indebtedness, and that the Grantor and its successors will warrant and defend title to the Grantee against the lawful claims of all persons. Taxes for the tax year of _____ shall be prorated between the Grantor and Grantee as of the date of recording of this deed.
Dated: _____

_____
Signature of Grantor

_____
Name of Grantor

_____   _____
Signature of Witness #1   Printed Name of Witness #1

_____   _____
Signature of Witness #2   Printed Name of Witness #2

State of _____
County of _____

On _____, the Grantor, _____
personally came before me and, being duly sworn, did state and prove that he/she is the person described in the above document and that he/she signed the above document in my presence.

_____
Notary Signature
Notary Public,
In and for the County of _____ State of _____
My commission expires: _____ Seal

Send all tax statements to Grantee.

Promissory Note (Installment Repayment)

$ _____

Dated: _____ , 20 _____

For value received,

_____ , Borrower,
address:

promises to pay
_____ , Noteholder,
address:

the principal amount of $ _____ , with interest at the annual rate of _____ percent, on any unpaid balance.

Payments are payable to the Noteholder in _____ consecutive installments of $ _____ , including interest, and continuing on the _____ day of each _____ until paid in full. If not paid off sooner, this note is due and payable in full on _____ , 20 _____ .

This note may be prepaid in whole or in part at any time without penalty. If the Borrower is in default more than _____ days with any payment, this note is payable upon demand of any Noteholder. This note is not assumable without the written consent of the Noteholder. The Borrower waives demand, presentment for payment, protest, and notice. In the event of any default, the Borrower will be responsible for any costs of collection on this note, including court costs and attorney fees.

_____
Signature of BORROWER

_____
Printed Name of Borrower

Promissory Note (Lump Sum Repayment)

$ _____

Dated: _____ , 20 _____

For value received,
_____ , Borrower,
address:

promises to pay
_____ , Noteholder,
address:

the principal amount of $ _____ , with interest at the annual rate of _____ percent, on any unpaid balance.

Payment on this note is due and payable to the Noteholder in full on or before
_____ , 20 _____ .

This note may be prepaid in whole or in part at any time without penalty. If the Borrower is in default more than _____ days with any payment, this note is payable upon demand of any Noteholder. This note is not assumable without the written consent of the Noteholder. The Borrower waives demand, presentment for payment, protest, and notice. In the event of any default, the Borrower will be responsible for any costs of collection on this note, including court costs and attorney fees.

_____
Signature of Borrower

_____
Printed Name of Borrower

Promissory Note (on Demand)

$ _____

Dated: _____, 20 _____

For value received,

_____ , Borrower,
address:

promises to pay ON DEMAND to
_____ , Noteholder,
address:

the principal amount of $ _____ , with interest at the annual rate of _____ percent, on any unpaid balance.

This note may be prepaid in whole or in part at any time without penalty. This note is not assumable without the written consent of the Noteholder. The Borrower waives demand, presentment for payment, protest, and notice. In the event of such default of over _____ days in making payment, the Borrower will be also be responsible for any costs of collection on this note, including court costs and attorney fees.

_____
Signature of Borrower

_____
Printed Name of Borrower

Release of Promissory Note

In consideration of full payment of the promissory note dated
_____ , 20 _____ , in the face amount of $ _____ ,
_____ , Noteholder,
address:

releases and discharges
_____ , Borrower(s),
address:

from any claims or obligations on account of this note.

The party signing this release intends that it bind and benefit both itself and any successors.

Dated: _____ , 20 _____

_____
Signature of Noteholder

_____
Printed Name of Noteholder

Comsewogue Public Library
170 Terryville Road
Port Jefferson Station, NY 11776